PETER RABBIT™ CROCHET TOYS

Adorable amigurumi from the
Tales of Beatrix Potter

Carla Mitrani

DAVID & CHARLES
—PUBLISHING—

www.davidandcharles.com

Contents

Introduction

Welcome to the world of Peter Rabbit and his friends! It makes me so happy to share with you my love for Beatrix Potter's characters. You see, Beatrix (am I allowed to use her first name?) and I go way back! When I was growing up in Buenos Aires, Argentina, I had all her illustrated books. When my father began to travel to London for work, he always brought me back as a gift a small porcelain figurine of one of Beatrix's characters, all of which I still treasure.

When my sons were born, their nursery room was decorated with framed watercolour paintings of Beatrix's drawings made by my aunt Carine, for she knew how much I loved Beatrix's art. And in July 2019, with my husband and the boys, we rented a motorhome and spent a vacation in her beloved Lake District. We even got to visit her farmhouse, Hill Top, which is featured in *The Tale of Tom Kitten*.

So you see, transforming Beatrix's drawings into crochet toys is a dream come true. I have tried to make them as easy and cuddly as possible so you can crochet them all and use them to recreate the many adventures and mischiefs Beatrix's imagination conjured up for them in her beautiful stories.

Are you ready? Let's start crocheting then!

THE TALE OF
BEATRIX POTTER'S
HILL TOP

Tools & materials

All the toys in this book were crocheted using cotton yarn. I crochet really tightly so that there are no gaps between the stitches and the stuffing won't show through. If you tend to crochet loosely, choose a smaller hook.

Yarn

I use only 100% cotton yarns because I like the feel and finish of cotton; it runs smoothly in your hands when working and it will not pill as acrylic or woollen yarns do. This means that the characters make more durable children's toys. Cotton also builds a sturdy, non-stretchy fabric, which will hold the stuffing without distorting the shape and volume of the bodies.

I used the following yarns:

- Scheepjes Cahlista (100% cotton), 10ply/aran, 85m (93yd) per 50g (1¾oz) ball
- Hobbii 8/8 Rainbow Cotton (100% cotton), 8ply/DK, 75m (82yd) per 50g (1¾oz) ball
- Hobbii 8/4 Rainbow Cotton (100% cotton), 4ply/fingering, 170m (186yd) per 50g (1¾oz) ball

How much yarn do I need?

Consider buying two 50g (1¾oz) balls of the fur or skin colour for the animals to be sure you have enough. For the clothes and accessories, depending on the size, just one ball is perfect. Even leftovers and scraps can come in handy for crocheting vegetables or small accessories.

Crochet hooks

Choose nicely built and comfortable hooks, since they will be your magic wands. The ones with ergonomic handles are really good to protect your hands and posture. My favourite ones are Clover Soft Touch. Most of the patterns use the 3mm (US C/2 or D/3) hook. The smaller hook is needed to crochet Mr. Jeremy Fisher, Mrs. Tittlemouse and certain accessories and you'll use the larger one for the watering can and pots.

- Size 3mm (US C/2 or D/3) hook
- Size 2.5mm (US B/1 or C/2) hook
- Size 4.5mm (US 7) hook

Other Tools and Materials

Stitch markers

When crocheting in a spiral, it's important to mark the beginning of each round with a stitch marker and move this stitch marker up as you work. You can use paper clips, hair clips, safety pins or even little scraps of yarn. Store them together in a small box or tin.

Toy safety eyes

Plastic, black, size 6mm (¼in) or 8mm (⅓in). For safety reasons, if you are planning to give the toy to a small child, you should embroider the eyes using black, dark grey or brown yarn instead.

Yarn/tapestry needle

Use this to sew the arms, legs, ears and other accessories to your animals. Find one with a blunt tip so it won't split the yarn, and an eye big enough to thread your choice of yarn through.

Scissors and seam ripper

Make sure your scissors are sharp. As for the seam ripper, keep it close: you might want to reposition something you've sewn in place – it's fine to remove it and start over!

Pins

These can be very helpful to hold certain pieces in place, like rabbit ears or tails, while you sew them on. Choose pins with coloured plastic or beaded heads so they won't slip inside the body and get lost.

Wooden chopstick

This is your secret weapon – there is nothing better than a broken chopstick to help spread out the stuffing evenly, and get it into complicated, hard-to-reach places.

Stuffing

Polyester fibrefill stuffing. You will need to stuff very firmly!

Pompom maker

This weird plastic contraption will help you create the pompons for the tails of the bunnies and Benjamin's tam-o-shanter. I use a Clover size 1⅝in (45mm). Or you can also use a fork for making them.

Craft bag and pencil case

The best thing about crochet is that you can take your current project everywhere, so be ready to pack your hooks, needles and yarns and continue your work in waiting rooms, on public transportation or in parks!

CROCHET STITCHES

ABBREVIATIONS

The patterns in this book are written using US crochet terms. These are listed here, along with their UK equivalents (where applicable):

beg	beginning
BLO	BLO
ch	chain stitch
dc	double crochet (UK treble crochet)
FLO	front loop only
hdc	half double crochet (UK half treble crochet)
pm	place marker
rep	repeat
sc	single crochet (UK double crochet)
sc2tog	single crochet 2 stitches together (UK double crochet 2 stitches together)
slst	slip stitch
st(s)	stitch(es)

STANDARD STITCHES

Slip knot

The slip knot is the starting point of the foundation chain and does not count as a stitch. Make a loop shape with the tail end of the yarn **(1)**. Insert the hook into it, yarn over hook and draw another loop through it **(2)**. Pull the yarn tail to tighten the loop around the hook **(3)**.

Chain stitch (ch)

Start with a slip knot, then yarn over hook **(4)**, pull through the loop on your hook **(5)** to create one chain stitch **(6)**. Repeat this as many times as stated in your pattern.

Slip stitch (slst)

Insert the hook into the stitch, yarn over hook **(7)**, pull through both the stitch and the loop on the hook at the same time **(8)**.

Single crochet (sc)

Insert the hook into the stitch, yarn over hook pull the yarn back through the stitch **(9)**. You will now have two loops on the hook **(10)**. Yarn over hook and draw it through both loops **(11)**.

Half double crochet (hdc)

Yarn over hook, insert the hook into the stitch **(12)**, yarn over hook again, pull the yarn through the stitch. You will have three loops on the hook **(13)**. Yarn over hook once more, pull through all three loops on the hook at once **(14)**.

Double crochet (dc)

Yarn over hook, insert the hook into the stitch **(15)**, yarn over hook again, pull the yarn through the stitch. You will have three loops on the hook **(16)**. Yarn over hook again, pull through the first two loops on the hook at once. You will now have two loops on the hook **(17)**. Yarn over hook once more, pull through both loops at once **(18)**.

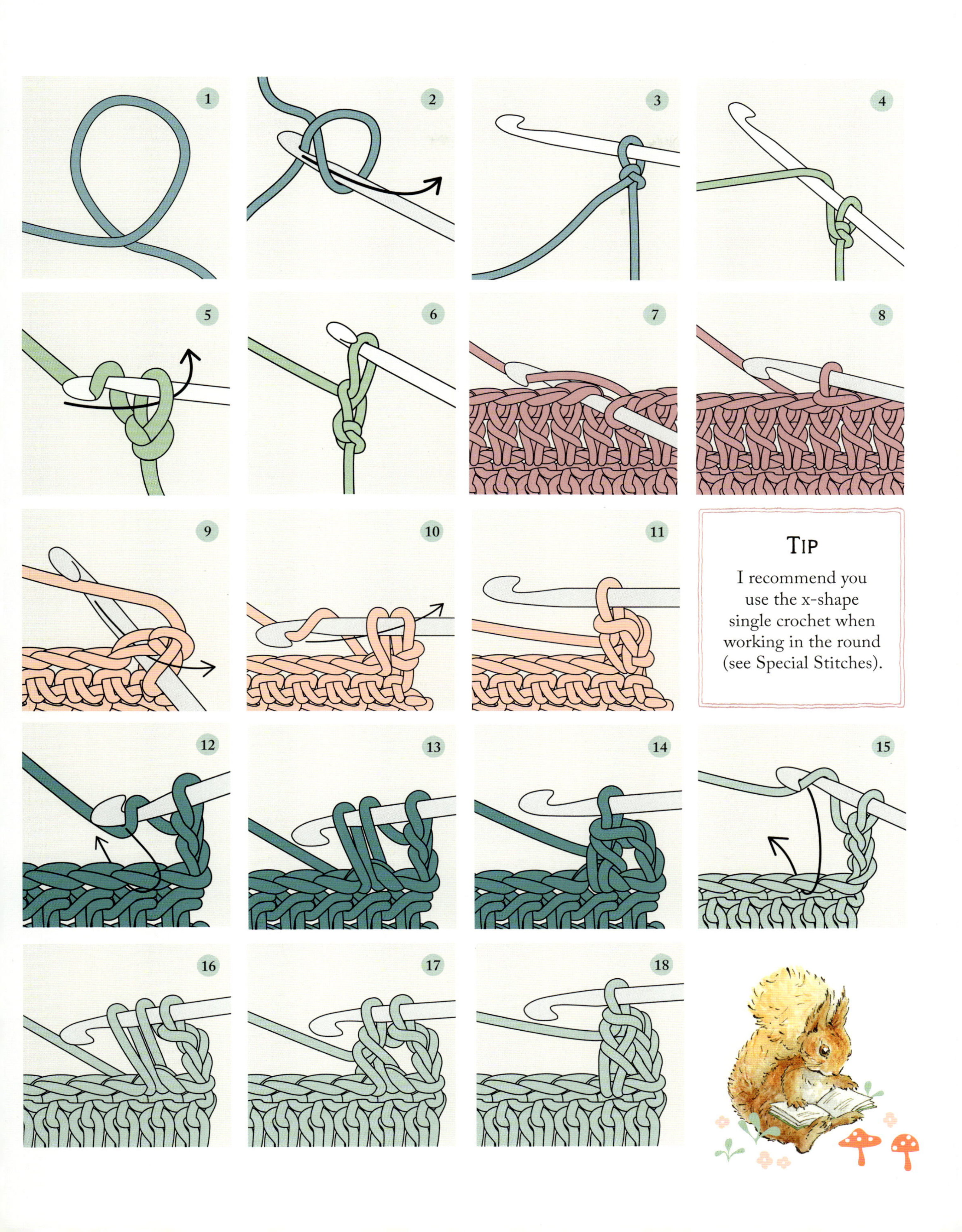

Tip

I recommend you use the x-shape single crochet when working in the round (see Special Stitches).

Special stitches

X-shape single crochet (sc)

Very (very) important: Throughout this book, for every animal and most accessories, I've used the x-shape sc. Why? Because when making x-shape single crochet your stitches will be tighter and will stand more on top of each other, which really makes a difference when the animals' bodies have multiple colour changes, like Peter, Benjamin, Flopsy or Tom Kitten. It's very easy to work the x-shape sc. Practise for a bit and I guarantee you'll love it! It goes like this:

Insert the hook into the stitch, yarn under hook **(1)** – so grab the yarn from above with the hook pointing down, instead of from below with the hook pointing up – pull the yarn back through the stitch. You will now have two loops on the hook. Yarn over hook **(2)** and draw it through both loops **(3)**.

Basket spike stitch

You'll use this stitch to crochet Mrs. Tiggy-Winkle's laundry basket. To achieve the desired effect, you work a traditional v-shaped sc (yarn over hook, not under). The basket effect is the result of alternating a single crochet made through the back loops of the previous round **(4)** with a single crochet spike stitch.

The spike stitch is worked as a sc into the stitch one round below the current round, into the same place where that stitch was worked. Insert hook one round below, yarn over hook, pull the yarn through the stitch and bring it to the height of the round you are working **(5)**. Yarn over hook again **(6)**, pull the yarn through both loops on your hook.

Tip

At first it might feel difficult to use the x-shape sc, but it will give a better look to colour changes.

PROJECTS

Peter Rabbit™

The Tale of Peter Rabbit was first published by Frederick Warne in 1902 and endures as Beatrix Potter's most popular and well-loved tale. It tells the story of a very mischievous rabbit and the trouble he encounters in Mr. McGregor's vegetable garden!

Materials

- 3mm (US C/2 or D/3) crochet hook
- 100% 8ply/DK cotton; colours used: golden-brown; nude; light blue; dark brown; white; a small amount of pale pink
- Stitch marker
- 8mm (⅓in) safety eyes
- Yarn needle
- Fibrefill stuffing
- 45mm (1⅝in) pompom maker

Finished size

20cm (7¾in) tall

Head

Round 1: Using golden-brown, 6 sc in a magic ring.

Round 2: 2 sc in each st. (12 sts)

Round 3: [1 sc, 2 sc in next st] to end. (18 sts)

Round 4: 1 sc, 2 sc in next st, [2 sc, 2 sc in next st] 5 times, 1 sc. (24 sts)

Round 5: [3 sc, 2 sc in next st] to end. (30 sts)

Round 6: 2 sc, 2 sc in next st, [4 sc, 2 sc in next st] 5 times, 2 sc. (36 sts)

Rounds 7–11: 1 sc in each st.

Round 12: [5 sc, 2 sc in next st] to end. (42 sts)

Rounds 13 and 14: 1 sc in each st.

On the next few rounds we will change colour several times. Remember to join the new colour in the last step of the previous st.

Round 15: 16 sc, change to nude, 4 sc, change to golden-brown, 5 sc, change to nude, 4 sc, change to golden-brown, 13 sc.

Round 16: 16 sc, change to nude, 2 sc in next st, 1 sc, 2 sc in next st, 1 sc, change to golden-brown, 2 sc in next st, 1 sc, 2 sc in next st, 1 sc, 2 sc in next st, change to nude, 1 sc, 2 sc in next st, 2 sc, change to golden-brown, 13 sc. (48 sts)

Round 17: 1 sc in each st.

Round 18: 20 sc, change to nude, 5 sc, change to golden-brown, 3 sc, change to nude, 5 sc, change to golden-brown, 15 sc.

Round 19: 17 sc, change to nude, 19 sc, change to golden-brown, 12 sc.

Round 20: 3 sc, sc2tog, 6 sc, sc2tog, 4 sc, change to nude, 2 sc, sc2tog, 6 sc, sc2tog, 7 sc, change to golden-brown, sc2tog, 5 sc, sc2tog, 3 sc. (42 sts)

Round 21: 5 sc, sc2tog, 5 sc, sc2tog, 1 sc, change to nude, 4 sc, sc2tog, 5 sc, sc2tog, 4 sc, change to golden-brown, 1 sc, sc2tog, 5 sc, sc2tog. (36 sts)

Round 22: 2 sc, sc2tog, 4 sc, sc2tog, 3 sc, change to nude, 1 sc, sc2tog, 4 sc, sc2tog, 4 sc, sc2tog, change to golden-brown, 4 sc, sc2tog, 2 sc. (30 sts)

Place safety eyes between Rounds 16 and 17, into the nude spots, with 9 sts between them. Embroider cheeks with pale pink. Using dark brown, embroider the nose and the details to the sides of the eyes, following the pictures as a guide **(1)**.

Round 23: 3 sc, sc2tog, 3 sc, sc2tog, 1 sc, change to nude, 2 sc, sc2tog, 3 sc, sc2tog, 3 sc, change to golden-brown, sc2tog, 3 sc, sc2tog. (24 sts)

Start stuffing the head at this point.

Round 24: 1 sc, sc2tog, 2 sc, sc2tog, 2 sc, change to nude, sc2tog, 2 sc, sc2tog, 2 sc, sc2tog, change to golden-brown, 2 sc, sc2tog, 1 sc. (18 sts)

Round 25: [1 sc, sc2tog] to end. (12 sts)

Round 26: [Sc2tog] 6 times. (6 sts)

Fasten off and close remaining sts through the front loops (see Techniques: Closing Remaining Stitches Through the Front Loops). Weave in ends (see Techniques: Hiding Ends Inside the Toy).

Body

Round 1: Using golden-brown, 6 sc in a magic ring.

Round 2: 2 sc in each st. (12 sts)

Round 3: 2 sc in each st. (24 sts)

Round 4: [3 sc, 2 sc in next st] to end. (30 sts)

Round 5: 2 sc, 2 sc in next st, [4 sc, 2 sc in next st] 5 times, 2 sc. (36 sts)

Round 6: [5 sc, 2 sc in next st] to end. (42 sts)

Rounds 7–10: 1 sc in each st.

Round 11: [5 sc, sc2tog] to end. (36 sts)

On the next few rounds we will change colour several times. Remember to join the new colour in the last step of the previous st.

Round 12: 15 sc, change to nude, 6 sc, change to golden-brown, 15 sc.

Rounds 13–16: 14 sc, change to nude, 8 sc, change to golden-brown, 14 sc.

Round 17: 2 sc, sc2tog, 4 sc, sc2tog, 4 sc, change to nude, sc2tog, 6 sc, change to golden-brown, sc2tog, 4 sc, sc2tog, 4 sc, sc2tog. (30 sts)

Rounds 18–20: 12 sc, change to nude, 7 sc, change to golden-brown, 11 sc.

Round 21: 3 sc, sc2tog, 3 sc, sc2tog, 2 sc, change to nude, 1 sc, sc2tog, 4 sc, change to golden-brown, sc2tog, 3 sc, sc2tog, 2 sc, sc2tog. (24 sts)

Start stuffing the body at this point.

Rounds 22 and 23: 10 sc, change to nude, 6 sc, change to golden-brown, 8 sc.

Round 24: 2 sc, sc2tog, 2 sc, sc2tog, 2 sc, change to nude, sc2tog, 4 sc, change to golden-brown, sc2tog, 1 sc, sc2tog, 1 sc, sc2tog. (18 sts)

Rounds 25 and 26: 8 sc, change to nude, 5 sc, change to golden-brown, 5 sc.

Fasten off, leaving a long tail for sewing to the head.

Arms (make two)

Round 1: Using golden-brown, ch 2, 4 sc in the second ch from hook. (4 sts)

Round 2: 2 sc in each st. (8 sts)

Rounds 3–14: 1 sc in each st.

There is no need to stuff the arms.

Press the opening together with your fingers with 4 sts on each side and join edges by working 1 sc into each pair of sts (see Techniques: Closing Limbs and Ears).

Fasten off, leaving a long tail for sewing to the body.

Ears (make two)

Round 1: Using golden-brown, 6 sc in a magic ring.

Round 2: 1 sc in each st.

Round 3: 2 sc in each st. (12 sts)

Rounds 4 and 5: 1 sc in each st.

On the next few rounds we will change colour several times. Remember to join the new colour in the last step of the previous st.

Round 6: 1 sc, change to nude, 2 sc in next st, 1 sc, change to golden-brown, 2 sc in next st, [1 sc, 2 sc in next st] 4 times. (18 sts)

Rounds 7–9: 1 sc, change to nude, 4 sc, change to golden-brown, 13 sc.

Round 10: 1 sc, change to nude, sc2tog, 2 sc, change to golden-brown, sc2tog, sc2tog, [1 sc, sc2tog] 3 times. (12 sts)

Rounds 11–13: 1 sc, change to nude, 3 sc, change to golden-brown, 8 sc.

Round 14: 1 sc in each st.

There is no need to stuff the ears.

Round 15: 1 sc. Leave remaining sts unworked.

Press the opening together with your fingers with 6 sts on each side and join edges by working 1 sc into each pair of sts.

Fasten off, leaving a long tail for sewing to the head **(2)**.

FEET (make two)

Round 1: Using golden-brown, ch 2, 4 sc in the second ch from hook. (4 sts)

Round 2: 2 sc in each st. (8 sts)

Rounds 3–6: 1 sc in each st.

There is no need to stuff the feet.

Press the opening together with your fingers with 4 sts on each side and join edges by working 1 sc into each pair of sts.

Fasten off, leaving a long tail for sewing to the body.

JACKET

This first part of the jacket will look like a vest and is worked in rows using light blue.

Row 1: Ch 21, 1 sc in the second ch from hook, 1 sc in each ch to end, ch 1, turn. (20 sts)

Row 2: 3 sc, ch 8, skip the following 4 sts (to create first armhole), 6 sc, ch 8, skip the following 4 sts (to create second armhole), 3 sc, ch 1, turn (see Techniques: Creating Armholes on Jackets).

Row 3: 3 sc, 1 sc FLO in each ch of 8-ch, 6 sc, 1 sc FLO in each ch of second 8-ch, 3 sc, ch 1, turn. (28 sts)

Rows 4–11: 1 sc in each st, ch 1, turn.

Row 12: Rotate the work 90 degrees clockwise and work 11 sc along the side of the vest, working in the spaces between rows. When you reach the top edge, work 20 sc in the remaining loops of the foundation chain. Then ch 1, rotate the piece 90 degrees clockwise again and work 11 sc along the other side of the vest, working in the spaces between rows (see Techniques: Edging Flat Pieces).

Fasten off and weave in ends (see Techniques: Weaving in Ends) **(3)**.

Sleeves

The sleeves of the jacket are worked in rounds.

Round 1: Join light blue in one of the remaining loops of the 8-ch from Row 2 of the vest, 1 sc in each remaining loop of ch, then 1 sc in each of the 4 sc you skipped before (see Techniques: Creating Sleeves). (12 sts)

Round 2: 1 sc in each st.

Round 3: [2 sc in next st, 5 sc] twice. (14 sts)

Round 4: 1 sc in each st.

Round 5: [2 sc in next st, 6 sc] twice. (16 sts)

Rounds 6–8: 1 sc in each st.

Round 9: 8 sc. Leave remaining sts unworked.

Fasten off and weave in ends.

Repeat these steps to crochet the other sleeve and weave in all ends.

Slippers (make two)

Round 1: Using dark brown, 5 sc in a magic ring.

Round 2: 2 sc in each st. (10 sts)

Rounds 3 and 4: 1 sc in each st.

Round 5: 4 sc, ch 1, turn. Leave remaining sts unworked.

Row 6: 1 sc in each st, ch 1, turn. (4 sts)

Row 7: 1 sc in each st.

Fasten off and weave in ends **(4)**.

Assembly

Pin the head to the body and then sew in place (see Techniques: Attaching Heads). When sewing through the nude part of the neck, work the needle through the back loops of the stitches so the golden-brown yarn doesn't show.

Sew the arms to the sides of the body between Rounds 23 and 24.

Curve the ears and sew them to the head between Rounds 6 and 7, counted from the magic ring on Round 1.

Sew the feet to the base of the body between Rounds 5 and 6.

Make a pompom with white and sew it to the back of the body.

Slip his arms into the sleeves of the jacket.

Weave in all ends inside the body.

Benjamin Bunny™

Peter Rabbit's cousin, Benjamin Bunny, has been a very popular character since his book's first publication in 1904. In this tale we hear all about his and Peter's adventures in Mr. McGregor's vegetable garden, and what happens to them when they meet a cat!

Materials

- 3mm (US C/2 or D/3) crochet hook
- 100% 8ply/DK cotton; colours used: golden-brown; nude; dark brown; light brown, dark green; white; bright red; a small amount of pale pink
- Stitch marker
- 8mm (⅓in) safety eyes
- Yarn needle
- Fibrefill stuffing
- 45mm (1⅝in) pompom maker

Finished size

20cm (7¾in) tall

Head

Round 1: Using golden-brown, 6 sc in a magic ring.

Round 2: 2 sc in each st. (12 sts)

Round 3: [1 sc, 2 sc in next st] to end. (18 sts)

Round 4: 1 sc, 2 sc in next st, [2 sc, 2 sc in next st] 5 times, 1 sc. (24 sts)

Round 5: [3 sc, 2 sc in next st] to end. (30 sts)

Round 6: 2 sc, 2 sc in next st, [4 sc, 2 sc in next st] 5 times, 2 sc. (36 sts)

Rounds 7–11: 1 sc in each st.

Rounds 12: [5 sc, 2 sc in next st] to end. (42 sts)

Rounds 13 and 14: 1 sc in each st.

On the next few rounds we will change colour several times. Remember to join the new colour in the last step of the previous st.

Round 15: 16 sc, change to nude, 4 sc, change to golden-brown, 5 sc, change to nude, 4 sc, change to golden-brown, 13 sc.

Round 16: 16 sc, change to nude, 2 sc in next st, 1 sc, 2 sc in next st, 1 sc, change to golden-brown, 2 sc in next st, 1 sc, 2 sc in next st, 1 sc, 2 sc in next st, change to nude, 1 sc, 2 sc in next st, 2 sc, change to golden-brown, 13 sc. (48 sts)

Round 17: 1 sc in each st.

Round 18: 20 sc, change to nude, 5 sc, change to golden-brown, 3 sc, change to nude, 5 sc, change to golden-brown, 15 sc.

Round 19: 17 sc, change to nude, 19 sc, change to golden-brown, 12 sc.

Round 20: 3 sc, sc2tog, 6 sc, sc2tog, 4 sc, change to nude, 2 sc, sc2tog, 6 sc, sc2tog, 7 sc, change to golden-brown, sc2tog, 5 sc, sc2tog, 3 sc. (42 sts)

Round 21: 5 sc, sc2tog, 5 sc, sc2tog, 1 sc, change to nude, 4 sc, sc2tog, 5 sc, sc2tog, 4 sc, change to golden-brown, 1 sc, sc2tog, 5 sc, sc2tog. (36 sts)

Round 22: 2 sc, sc2tog, 4 sc, sc2tog, 3 sc, change to nude, 1 sc, sc2tog, 4 sc, sc2tog, 4 sc, sc2tog, change to golden-brown, 4 sc, sc2tog, 2 sc. (30 sts)

Place safety eyes between Rounds 16 and 17, into the nude spots, with 9 sts between them. Embroider cheeks with pale pink. Using dark brown, embroider the nose and the details to the sides of the eyes, following the pictures as a guide.

Round 23: 3 sc, sc2tog, 3 sc, sc2tog, 1 sc, change to nude, 2 sc, sc2tog, 3 sc, sc2tog, 3 sc, change to golden-brown, sc2tog, 3 sc, sc2tog. (24 sts)

Start stuffing the head at this point.

Round 24: 1 sc, sc2tog, 2 sc, sc2tog, 2 sc, change to nude, sc2tog, 2 sc, sc2tog, 2 sc, sc2tog, change to golden-brown, 2 sc, sc2tog, 1 sc. (18 sts)

Round 25: [1 sc, sc2tog] to end. (12 sts)

Round 26: [Sc2tog] 6 times. (6 sts)

Fasten off and close remaining sts through the front loops (see Techniques: Closing Remaining Stitches Through the Front Loops). Weave in ends (see Techniques: Hiding Ends Inside the Toy).

Body

Round 1: Using golden-brown, 6 sc in a magic ring.

Round 2: 2 sc in each st. (12 sts)

Round 3: 2 sc in each st. (24 sts)

Round 4: [3 sc, 2 sc in next st] to end. (30 sts)

Round 5: 2 sc, 2 sc in next st, [4 sc, 2 sc in next st] 5 times, 2 sc. (36 sts)

Round 6: [5 sc, 2 sc in next st] to end. (42 sts)

Rounds 7–10: 1 sc in each st.

Round 11: [5 sc, sc2tog] to end. (36 sts)

On the next few rounds we will change colour several times. Remember to join the new colour in the last step of the previous st.

Round 12: 15 sc, change to nude, 6 sc, change to golden-brown, 15 sc.

Rounds 13–16: 14 sc, change to nude, 8 sc, change to golden-brown, 14 sc.

Round 17: 2 sc, sc2tog, 4 sc, sc2tog, 4 sc, change to nude, sc2tog, 6 sc, change to golden-brown, sc2tog, 4 sc, sc2tog, 4 sc, sc2tog. (30 sts)

Rounds 18–20: 12 sc, change to nude, 7 sc, change to golden-brown, 11 sc.

Round 21: 3 sc, sc2tog, 3 sc, sc2tog, 2 sc, change to nude, 1 sc, sc2tog, 4 sc, change to golden-brown, sc2tog, 3 sc, sc2tog, 2 sc, sc2tog. (24 sts)

Start stuffing the body at this point.

Rounds 22 and 23: 10 sc, change to nude, 6 sc, change to golden-brown, 8 sc.

Round 24: 2 sc, sc2tog, 2 sc, sc2tog, 2 sc, change to nude, sc2tog, 4 sc, change to golden-brown, sc2tog, 1 sc, sc2tog, 1 sc, sc2tog. (18 sts)

Rounds 25 and 26: 8 sc, change to nude, 5 sc, change to golden-brown, 5 sc.

Fasten off, leaving a long tail for sewing to the head.

Arms (make two)

Round 1: Using golden-brown, ch 2, 4 sc in the second ch from hook. (4 sts)

Round 2: 2 sc in each st. (8 sts)

Rounds 3–14: 1 sc in each st.

There is no need to stuff the arms.

Press the opening together with your fingers with 4 sts on each side and join edges by working 1 sc into each pair of sts (see Techniques: Closing Limbs and Ears).

Fasten off, leaving a long tail for sewing to the body.

Ears (make two)

Round 1: Using golden-brown, 6 sc in a magic ring.

Round 2: 1 sc in each st.

Round 3: 2 sc in each st. (12 sts)

Rounds 4 and 5: 1 sc in each st.

On the next few rounds we will change colour several times. Remember to join the new colour in the last step of the previous st.

Round 6: 1 sc, change to nude, 2 sc in next st, 1 sc, change to golden-brown, 2 sc in next st, [1 sc, 2 sc in next st] 4 times. (18 sts)

Rounds 7–9: 1 sc, change to nude, 4 sc, change to golden-brown, 13 sc.

Round 10: 1 sc, change to nude, sc2tog, 2 sc, change to golden-brown, sc2tog, sc2tog, [1 sc, sc2tog] 3 times. (12 sts)

Rounds 11–13: 1 sc, change to nude, 3 sc, change to golden-brown, 8 sc.

Round 14: 1 sc in each st.

There is no need to stuff the ears.

Round 15: 1 sc. Leave remaining sts unworked.

Press the opening together with your fingers with 6 sts on each side and join edges by working 1 sc into each pair of sts.

Fasten off, leaving a long tail for sewing to the head **(1)**.

Feet (make two)

Round 1: Using golden-brown, ch 2, 4 sc in second ch from hook. (4 sts)

Round 2: 2 sc in each st. (8 sts)

Rounds 3–6: 1 sc in each st.

There is no need to stuff the feet.

Press the opening together with your fingers with 4 sts on each side and join edges by working 1 sc into each pair of sts.

Fasten off, leaving a long tail for sewing to the body.

Jacket

This first part of the jacket will look like a vest and is worked in rows using light brown.

Row 1: Ch 21, 1 sc in the second ch from hook, 1 sc in each ch to end, ch 1, turn. (20 sts)

Row 2: 3 sc, ch 8, skip the following 4 sts (to create first armhole), 6 sc, ch 8, skip the following 4 sts (to create second armhole), 3 sc, ch 1, turn (see Techniques: Creating Armholes on Jackets).

Row 3: 3 sc, 1 sc FLO in each ch of 8-ch, 6 sc, 1 sc FLO in each ch of second 8-ch, 3 sc, ch 1, turn. (28 sts)

Rows 4–11: 1 sc in each st, ch 1, turn.

Row 12: Rotate the work 90 degrees clockwise and work 11 sc along the side of the vest, working in the spaces between rows. When you reach the top edge, work 20 sc in the remaining loops of the foundation chain. Then ch 1, rotate the piece 90 degrees clockwise again and work 11 sc along the other side of the vest, working in the spaces between rows (see Techniques: Edging Flat Pieces).

Fasten off and weave in ends (see Techniques: Weaving in Ends).

Sleeves

The sleeves of the jacket are worked in rounds.

Round 1: Join light brown in one of the remaining loops of the 8-ch from Row 2 of the vest **(2)**, 1 sc in each remaining loop of ch, then 1 sc in each of the 4 sc you skipped before (see Techniques: Creating Sleeves). (12 sts)

Round 2: 1 sc in each st.

Round 3: [2 sc in next st, 5 sc] twice. (14 sts)

Round 4: 1 sc in each st.

Round 5: [2 sc in next st, 6 sc] twice. (16 sts)

Rounds 6–8: 1 sc in each st.

Round 9: 8 sc. Leave remaining sts unworked.

Fasten off and weave in ends.

Repeat these steps to crochet the other sleeve **(3)**.

SLIPPERS (make two)

Round 1: Using dark brown, 5 sc in a magic ring.

Round 2: 2 sc in each st. (10 sts)

Rounds 3 and 4: 1 sc in each st.

Row 5: 4 sc, ch 1, turn. Leave remaining sts unworked.

Row 6: 1 sc in each st, ch 1, turn. (4 sts)

Row 7: 1 sc in each st.

Fasten off and weave in ends.

TAM-O-SHANTER

Round 1: Using dark green, 6 sc in a magic ring.

Round 2: 2 sc in each st. (12 sts)

Round 3: 2 sc in each st. (24 sts)

Round 4: [3 sc, 2 sc in next st] to end. (30 sts)

Round 5: Ch 8, skip the following 4 sts (to create first ear hole), 11 sc, ch 8, skip the following 4 sts (to create second ear hole), 11 sc **(4)**.

Round 6: [1 sc FLO in each ch of 8-ch, 11 sc] twice. (38 sts)

Round 7: 8 sc, 2 sc in next st, 18 sc, 2 sc in next st, 10 sc. (40 sts)

Round 8: [1 sc, 2 sc in next st] to end. (60 sts)

Round 9: [2 sc, 2 sc in next st] to end. (80 sts)

Rounds 10–14: 1 sc in each st.

Round 15: [2 sc, sc2tog] to end. (60 sts)

Round 16: [1 sc, sc2tog] to end. (40 sts)

Fasten off and weave in ends.

ASSEMBLY

Pin the head to the body and sew in place (see Techniques: Attaching Heads). When sewing through the nude part of the neck, work the needle through the back loops of the stitches, so the golden-brown yarn doesn't show.

Sew the arms to the sides of the body between Rounds 23 and 24.

Curve the ears and sew them to the head between Rounds 6 and 7, counted from the magic ring on Round 1.

Sew the feet to the base of the body between Rounds 5 and 6.

Make a pompom with white and sew it to the back of the body.

Slip his arms through the sleeves of the jacket.

Make a pompom with bright red and sew it to the tam-o-shanter **(5)**, then place it on his head, passing the ears through the holes.

Put the slippers on his feet. You can sew them in place if you don't want him to lose them like Peter does in the story.

Weave in all ends inside the body.

FLOPSY™

When the cupboard is bare at Flopsy and Benjamin's burrow, the family all have to go in search of food. They soon find some old lettuces on Mr. McGregor's rubbish heap, but who can imagine the horrors that await them as they enjoy a nap after lunch!

Materials

- 3mm (US C/2 or D/3) crochet hook
- 100% 8ply/DK cotton; colours used: golden-brown; nude; white; pale pink; a small amount of dark brown
- Stitch marker
- 8mm (⅓in) safety eyes
- Yarn needle
- Fibrefill stuffing
- 45mm (1⅝in) pompom maker

Finished size

20cm (7¾in) tall

Head

Round 1: Using golden-brown, 6 sc in a magic ring.

Round 2: 2 sc in each st. (12 sts)

Round 3: [1 sc, 2 sc in next st] to end. (18 sts)

Round 4: 1 sc, 2 sc in next st, [2 sc, 2 sc in next st] 5 times, 1 sc. (24 sts)

Round 5: [3 sc, 2 sc in next st] to end. (30 sts)

Round 6: 2 sc, 2 sc in next st, [4 sc, 2 sc in next st] 5 times, 2 sc. (36 sts)

Rounds 7–11: 1 sc in each st.

Rounds 12: [5 sc, 2 sc in next st] to end. (42 sts)

Rounds 13 and 14: 1 sc in each st.

On the next few rounds we change colour several times. Remember to join the new colour in the last step of the previous st.

Round 15: 16 sc, change to nude, 4 sc, change to golden-brown, 5 sc, change to nude, 4 sc, change to golden-brown, 13 sc.

Round 16: 16 sc, change to nude, 2 sc in next st, 1 sc, 2 sc in next st, 1 sc, change to golden-brown, 2 sc in next st, 1 sc, 2 sc in next st, 1 sc, 2 sc in next st, change to nude, 1 sc, 2 sc in next st, 2 sc, change to golden-brown, 13 sc. (48 sts)

Round 17: 1 sc in each st.

Round 18: 20 sc, change to nude, 5 sc, change to golden-brown, 3 sc, change to nude, 5 sc, change to golden-brown, 15 sc.

Round 19: 17 sc, change to nude, 19 sc, change to golden-brown, 12 sc.

Round 20: 3 sc, sc2tog, 6 sc, sc2tog, 4 sc, change to nude, 2 sc, sc2tog, 6 sc, sc2tog, 7 sc, change to golden-brown, sc2tog, 5 sc, sc2tog, 3 sc. (42 sts)

Round 21: 5 sc, sc2tog, 5 sc, sc2tog, 1 sc, change to nude, 4 sc, sc2tog, 5 sc, sc2tog, 4 sc, change to golden-brown, 1 sc, sc2tog, 5 sc, sc2tog. (36 sts)

Round 22: 2 sc, sc2tog, 4 sc, sc2tog, 3 sc, change to nude, 1 sc, sc2tog, 4 sc, sc2tog, 4 sc, sc2tog, change to golden-brown, 4 sc, sc2tog, 2 sc. (30 sts)

Place safety eyes between Rounds 16 and 17, into the nude spots, with 9 sts between them. Embroider cheeks with pale pink. Using dark brown embroider the nose, and then a pair of eyelashes to the side of each eye, following the pictures as a guide **(1)**.

Round 23: 3 sc, sc2tog, 3 sc, sc2tog, 1 sc, change to nude, 2 sc, sc2tog, 3 sc, sc2tog, 3 sc, change to golden-brown, sc2tog, 3 sc, sc2tog. (24 sts)

Start stuffing the head at this point.

Round 24: 1 sc, sc2tog, 2 sc, sc2tog, 2 sc, change to nude, sc2tog, 2 sc, sc2tog, 2 sc, sc2tog, change to golden-brown, 2 sc, sc2tog, 1 sc. (18 sts)

Round 25: [1 sc, sc2tog] to end. (12 sts)

Round 26: [Sc2tog] 6 times. (6 sts)

Fasten off and close remaining sts through the front loops (see Techniques: Closing Remaining Stitches Through the Front Loops). Weave in ends (see Techniques: Hiding Ends Inside the Toy).

Body

Round 1: Using golden-brown, 6 sc in a magic ring.

Round 2: 2 sc in each st. (12 sts)

Round 3: 2 sc in each st. (24 sts)

Round 4: [3 sc, 2 sc in next st] to end. (30 sts)

Round 5: 2 sc, 2 sc in next st, [4 sc, 2 sc in next st] 5 times, 2 sc. (36 sts)

Round 6: [5 sc, 2 sc in next st] to end. (42 sts)

Rounds 7–10: 1 sc in each st.

Round 11: [5 sc, sc2tog] to end. (36 sts)

On the next few rounds we will change colour several times. Remember to join the new colour in the last step of the previous st.

Round 12: 15 sc, change to nude, 6 sc, change to golden-brown, 15 sc.

Rounds 13–16: 14 sc, change to nude, 8 sc, change to golden-brown, 14 sc.

Round 17: 2 sc, sc2tog, 4 sc, sc2tog, 4 sc, change to nude, sc2tog, 6 sc, change to golden-brown, sc2tog, 4 sc, sc2tog, 4 sc, sc2tog. (30 sts)

Rounds 18–20: 12 sc, change to nude, 7 sc, change to golden-brown, 11 sc.

Round 21: 3 sc, sc2tog, 3 sc, sc2tog, 2 sc, change to nude, 1 sc, sc2tog, 4 sc, change to golden-brown, sc2tog, 3 sc, sc2tog, 2 sc, sc2tog. (24 sts)

Start stuffing the body at this point.

Rounds 22 and 23: 10 sc, change to nude, 6 sc, change to golden-brown, 8 sc.

Round 24: 2 sc, sc2tog, 2 sc, sc2tog, 2 sc, change to nude, sc2tog, 4 sc, change to golden-brown, sc2tog, 1 sc, sc2tog, 1 sc, sc2tog. (18 sts)

Rounds 25 and 26: 8 sc, change to nude, 5 sc, change to golden-brown, 5 sc.

Fasten off, leaving a long tail for sewing to the head.

Arms (make two)

Round 1: Using golden-brown, ch 2, 4 sc in the second ch from hook. (4 sts)

Round 2: 2 sc in each st. (8 sts)

Rounds 3–14: 1 sc in each st.

There is no need to stuff the arms.

Press the opening together with your fingers with 4 sts on each side and join edges by working 1 sc into each pair of sts (see Techniques: Closing Limbs and Ears).

Fasten off, leaving a long tail for sewing to the body.

Ears (make two)

Round 1: Using golden-brown, 6 sc in a magic ring.

Round 2: 1 sc in each st.

Round 3: 2 sc in each st. (12 sts)

Rounds 4 and 5: 1 sc in each st.

On the next few rounds we will change colour several times. Remember to join the new colour in the last step of the previous st.

Round 6: 1 sc, change to nude, 2 sc in next st, 1 sc, change to golden-brown, 2 sc in next st, [1 sc, 2 sc in next st] 4 times. (18 sts)

Rounds 7–9: 1 sc, change to nude, 4 sc, change to golden-brown, 13 sc.

Round 10: 1 sc, change to nude, sc2tog, 2 sc, change to golden-brown, sc2tog, sc2tog, [1 sc, sc2tog] 3 times. (12 sts)

Rounds 11–13: 1 sc, change to nude, 3 sc, change to golden-brown, 8 sc.

Round 14: 1 sc in each st.

There is no need to stuff the ears.

Round 15: 1 sc. Leave remaining sts unworked.

Press the opening together with your fingers with 6 sts on each side and join edges by working 1 sc into each pair of sts.

Fasten off, leaving a long tail for sewing to the head **(2)**.

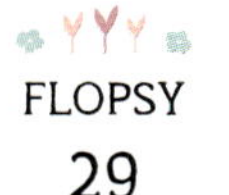

FEET (make two)

Round 1: Using golden-brown, ch 2, 4 sc in the second ch from hook. (4 sts)

Round 2: 2 sc in each st. (8 sts)

Rounds 3–6: 1 sc in each st.

There is no need to stuff the feet.

Press the opening together with your fingers with 4 sts on each side and join edges by working 1 sc into each pair of sts.

Fasten off, leaving a long tail for sewing to the body.

CAPE

The cape is worked in rows using pale pink.

Row 1: Leaving a long initial tail, ch 14, 1 hdc in the third ch from hook, 3 hdc, 4 sc, 4 slst, ch 1, turn. (12 sts)

Row 2: 4 slst BLO, 4 sc BLO, 4 hdc BLO **(3)**, turn.

Row 3: Ch 2 (does not count as a st), 4 hdc BLO, 4 sc BLO, 4 slst BLO, ch 1, turn.

Rows 4–35: Repeat Rows 2 and 3 another 16 times.

Fasten off, leaving a long tail for tying around the neck **(4)**.

ASSEMBLY

Pin the head to the body and sew in place (see Techniques: Attaching Heads). When sewing through the nude part of the neck, work the needle through the back loops of the stitches, so the golden-brown yarn doesn't show.

Sew the arms to the sides of the body between Rounds 23 and 24.

Curve the ears and sew one to the head between Rounds 6 and 7, counted from the magic ring on Round 1, and the other between Rounds 5 and 6, so it tilts to the side.

Sew the feet to the base of the body between Rounds 5 and 6.

Make a pompom with white and sew it to the back of the body.

Weave in all ends inside the body.

Tie the cape around Flopsy's neck.

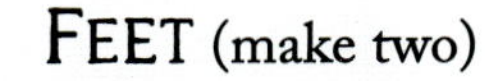

Watering Can, Pots & Veggies

Peter Rabbit enjoys eating lettuces, French beans and radishes in Mr. McGregor's garden and after escaping Mr. McGregor's clutches, he takes refuge in the tool-shed where there are lots of pots to hide under – but Peter chooses a watering can that's full of water!

Materials

- 4.5mm (US 7) crochet hook
- 100% 8ply/DK cotton held double; colours used: sage green
- Stitch marker
- Yarn needle
- 35 x 10cm (13¾ x 4in) piece of cardboard

Finished size

20cm (7¾in) tall

Watering can body

Round 1: Using 2 strands of sage green held together, 6 sc in a magic ring.

Round 2: 2 sc in each st. (12 sts)

Round 3: 2 sc in each st. (24 sts)

Round 4: [3 sc, 2 sc in next st] to end. (30 sts)

Round 5: 2 sc, 2 sc in next st, [4 sc, 2 sc in next st] 5 times, 2 sc. (36 sts)

Round 6: [5 sc, 2 sc in next st] to end. (42 sts)

Round 7: [2 sc, 2 sc in next st] to end. (56 sts)

Round 8: [13 sc, 2 sc in next st] to end. (60 sts)

Round 9: 1 sc BLO in each st.

Rounds 10–13: 1 sc in each st.

Round 14: 1 sc BLO in each st.

Rounds 15–25: 1 sc in each st.

Round 26: 1 sc BLO in each st.

Rounds 27–30: 1 sc in each st.

Fasten off (see Techniques: Weaving in Ends).

Half lid

Row 1: Using 2 strands of sage green held together, 6 sc in a magic ring, ch 1, turn.

Row 2: 2 sc in each st, ch 1, turn. (12 sts)

Row 3: 1 sc in each st, ch 1, turn.

Row 4: 3 sc, 2 sc in next st, 4 sc, 2 sc in next st, 3 sc, ch 1, turn. (14 sts)

Row 5: [1 sc, 2 sc in next st] to end, ch 1, turn. (21 sts)

Row 6: 1 sc in each st, ch 1, turn.

Row 7: [2 sc, 2 sc in next st] to end, ch 1, turn. (28 sts)

Row 8: 1 sc in each st, ch 1, turn.

Row 9: 14 sc along the flat edge, working into the spaces between rounds **(1)**. (14 sts)

Fasten off, leaving a long tail for sewing to the can.

TOP HANDLE

Row 1: Using 2 strands of sage green held together, ch 41, 1 sc in the second ch from hook, 1 sc in each ch to end, ch 1, turn. (40 sts)

Row 2: 1 sc in each st, ch 1, turn.

Row 3: 1 sc in each st.

Fasten off, leaving a long tail for sewing to the can.

SIDE HANDLE

Row 1: Using 2 strands of sage green held together, ch 31, 1 sc in the second ch from hook, 1 sc in each ch to end, ch 1, turn. (30 sts)

Row 2: 1 sc in each st, ch 1, turn.

Row 3: 1 sc in each st.

Fasten off, leaving a long tail for sewing to the can.

SPOUT

Round 1: Using 2 strands of sage green held together, 6 sc in a magic ring.

Round 2: 2 sc in each st. (12 sts)

Round 3: 2 sc in each st. (24 sts)

Round 4: [3 sc, 2 sc in next st] to end. (30 sts)

Round 5: 2 sc, 2 sc in next st, [4 sc, 2 sc in next st] 5 times, 2 sc. (36 sts)

Round 6: 1 sc BLO in each st.

Round 7: 2 sc, sc2tog, [4 sc, sc2tog] 5 times, 2 sc. (30 sts)

Round 8: 1 sc in each st.

Round 9: [3 sc, sc2tog] to end. (24 sts)

Round 10: 1 sc in each st.

Round 11: 1 sc, sc2tog, [2 sc, sc2tog] 5 times, 1 sc. (18 sts)

Stuff firmly.

Round 12: 1 sc in each st.

Round 13: [1 sc, sc2tog] to end. (12 sts)

Rounds 14–26: 1 sc in each st.

Round 27: 1 sc, 6 hdc, 1 sc, 4 slst.

Round 28: 1 sc, 6 hdc, 1 sc. Leave remaining sts unworked.

Fasten off, leaving a long tail for sewing to the can **(2)**.

SPOUT SUPPORT

Row 1: Using 2 strands of sage green held together, ch 7, 1 sc in the second ch from hook, 1 sc in each ch to end. (6 sts)

Fasten off, leaving a long tail for sewing to the can.

ASSEMBLY

Sew the half lid to the opening of the can.

Sew the top handle over the can and the side handle to the side, opposite the half lid.

Sew the spout to the side, opposite the side handle, and secure it in place with the support.

Weave in all ends and place the piece of cardboard inside the watering can, around the inside edges.

1

2

Materials

- 4.5mm (US 7) crochet hook
- 100% 8ply/DK cotton held double; colours used: burnt orange
- Stitch marker
- Yarn needle

Finished size

Large pot: 10cm (4in) tall

Small pot: 9cm (3½in) tall

Large pot

Round 1: Using 2 strands of burnt orange held together, 6 sc in a magic ring.

Round 2: 2 sc in each st. (12 sts)

Round 3: 2 sc in each st **(1)**. (24 sts)

Round 4: [3 sc, 2 sc in next st] to end. (30 sts)

Round 5: 2 sc, 2 sc in next st, [4 sc, 2 sc in next st] 5 times, 2 sc. (36 sts)

Round 6: [5 sc, 2 sc in next st] to end. (42 sts)

Round 7: [2 sc, 2 sc in next st] to end. (56 sts)

Round 8: 1 sc BLO in each st.

Rounds 9–12: 1 sc in each st.

Round 13: [13 sc, 2 sc in next st] to end. (60 sts)

Rounds 14–17: 1 sc in each st.

Round 18: 7 sc, 2 sc in next st, [14 sc, 2 sc in next st] 3 times, 7 sc. (64 sts)

Rounds 19–22: 1 sc in each st.

Round 23: [15 sc, 2 sc in next st] to end. (68 sts)

Round 24: 1 sc in each st.

Fasten off invisibly (see Techniques: Fastening off Invisibly) and weave in ends (see Techniques: Weaving in Ends).

Pot edge

Turn the pot upside down and join 2 strands of burnt orange held together in one of the front loops of the last round **(2)**.

Round 1: 1 sc FLO in each st. (68 sts)

Rounds 2–5: 1 sc in each st.

Fasten off invisibly and weave in ends **(3)**.

SMALL POT

Round 1: Using 2 strands of burnt orange held together, 6 sc in a magic ring.

Round 2: 2 sc in each st. (12 sts)

Round 3: 2 sc in each st. (24 sts)

Round 4: [3 sc, 2 sc in next st] to end. (30 sts)

Round 5: 2 sc, 2 sc in next st, [4 sc, 2 sc in next st] 5 times, 2 sc. (36 sts)

Round 6: [5 sc, 2 sc in next st] to end. (42 sts)

Round 7: 1 sc BLO in each st.

Rounds 8–10: 1 sc in each st.

Round 11: [13 sc, 2 sc in next st] to end. (45 sts)

Rounds 12–14: 1 sc in each st.

Round 15: 7 sc, 2 sc in next st, [14 sc, 2 sc in next st] twice, 7 sc. (48 sts)

Rounds 16–18: 1 sc in each st.

Round 19: [11 sc, 2 sc in next st] to end. (52 sts)

Round 20: 1 sc in each st.

Fasten off invisibly and weave in ends.

POT EDGE

Turn the pot upside down and join 2 strands of burnt orange held together in one of the front loops of the last round.

Round 1: 1 sc FLO in each st. (52 sts)

Rounds 2–4: 1 sc in each st.

Fasten off invisibly and weave in ends.

1

2

3

Materials

- 2.5mm (US B/1 or C/2) crochet hook
- 100% 4ply/fingering cotton; colours used:
- For the radishes: white; dark pink; sage green
- For the cabbage: light green
- For the carrots: orange; burnt orange; light green; sage green
- Stitch marker
- Yarn needle
- Fibrefill stuffing

Finished size

Radish: 6cm (2½in) tall

Cabbage: 2.5cm (1in) tall

Carrot: 6cm (2½in) tall

Radish

Round 1: Using white, 6 sc in a magic ring.

Round 2: 1 sc in each st.

Round 3: Change to dark pink, 1 sc in each st.

Round 4: 2 sc in each st. (12 sts)

Round 5: [1 sc, 2 sc in next st] to end. (18 sts)

Rounds 6–9: 1 sc in each st.

Stuff firmly.

Round 10: [1 sc, sc2tog] to end. (12 sts)

Round 11: [Sc2tog] 6 times. (6 sts)

Fasten off and close remaining sts through the front loops (see Techniques: Closing Remaining Stitches Through the Front Loops). Weave in ends (see Techniques: Hiding Ends Inside the Toy).

Radish leaves (make two)

Round 1: Using sage green, ch 11, starting in the second ch from hook, 4 slst, 1 sc, 1 hdc, 1 dc, 1 hdc, 1 sc, 3 slst in the last st (this will allow you to work on the other side of the chain), 1 sc, 1 hdc, 1 dc, 1 hdc, 1 sc, 4 slst. (21 sts)

Fasten off, leaving a long tail for sewing to the radish **(1)**.

Cabbage heart

Round 1: Using light green, 6 sc in a magic ring.

Round 2: 2 sc in each st. (12 sts)

Round 3: [1 sc, 2 sc in next st] to end. (18 sts)

Round 4: 1 sc, 2 sc in next st, [2 sc, 2 sc in next st] 5 times, 1 sc. (24 sts)

Rounds 5–9: 1 sc in each st.

Stuff firmly.

Round 10: 1 sc, sc2tog, [2 sc, sc2tog] 5 times, 1 sc. (18 sts)

Round 11: [1 sc, sc2tog] to end. (12 sts)

Round 12: [Sc2tog] 6 times. (6 sts)

Fasten off and close remaining sts through the front loops. Weave in ends (see Techniques: Weaving in Ends).

Cabbage leaves (make six)

Round 1: Using light green, ch 5, starting in the second ch from hook, 3 sc, 4 sc in the last st (this will allow you to work on the other side of the chain), 3 sc, ch 1, turn. (10 sts)

Round 2: 3 sc, [2 sc in next st] 4 times, 3 sc, ch 1, turn. (14 sts)

Round 3: 5 sc, 2 sc in next st, 3 sc, 2 sc in next st, 4 sc, ch 1, turn. (16 sts)

Round 4: [5 sc, 2 sc in next st] twice, 4 sc. (18 sts)

Fasten off, leaving a long tail for sewing to the cabbage.

Carrot

Round 1: Using orange or burnt orange, 6 sc in a magic ring.

Rounds 2 and 3: 1 sc in each st.

Round 4: [1 sc, 2 sc in next st] to end. (9 sts)

Rounds 5–7: 1 sc in each st.

Round 8: 1 sc, 2 sc in next st, [2 sc, 2 sc in next st] twice, 1 sc. (12 sts)

Rounds 9–11: 1 sc in each st.

Stuff firmly.

Round 12: [Sc2tog] 6 times. (6 sts)

Fasten off and close remaining sts through the front loops. Weave in ends.

Carrot leaves (make two)

Round 1: Using light green or sage green, ch 11, 1 hdc in the third ch from hook, 2 hdc, 3 sc, 3 slst. (9 sts)

Fasten off, leaving a long tail for sewing to the carrot.

Assembly

Sew the radish leaves to the middle of the magic ring on Round 1 of the radish **(2)**.

Weave in all ends.

Arrange the cabbage leaves around the centre of the cabbage, slightly overlapping them. Secure the position with pins **(3)** and then sew them in place, one by one. Weave in all ends.

Sew two leaves to each carrot and weave in ends.

1

2

3

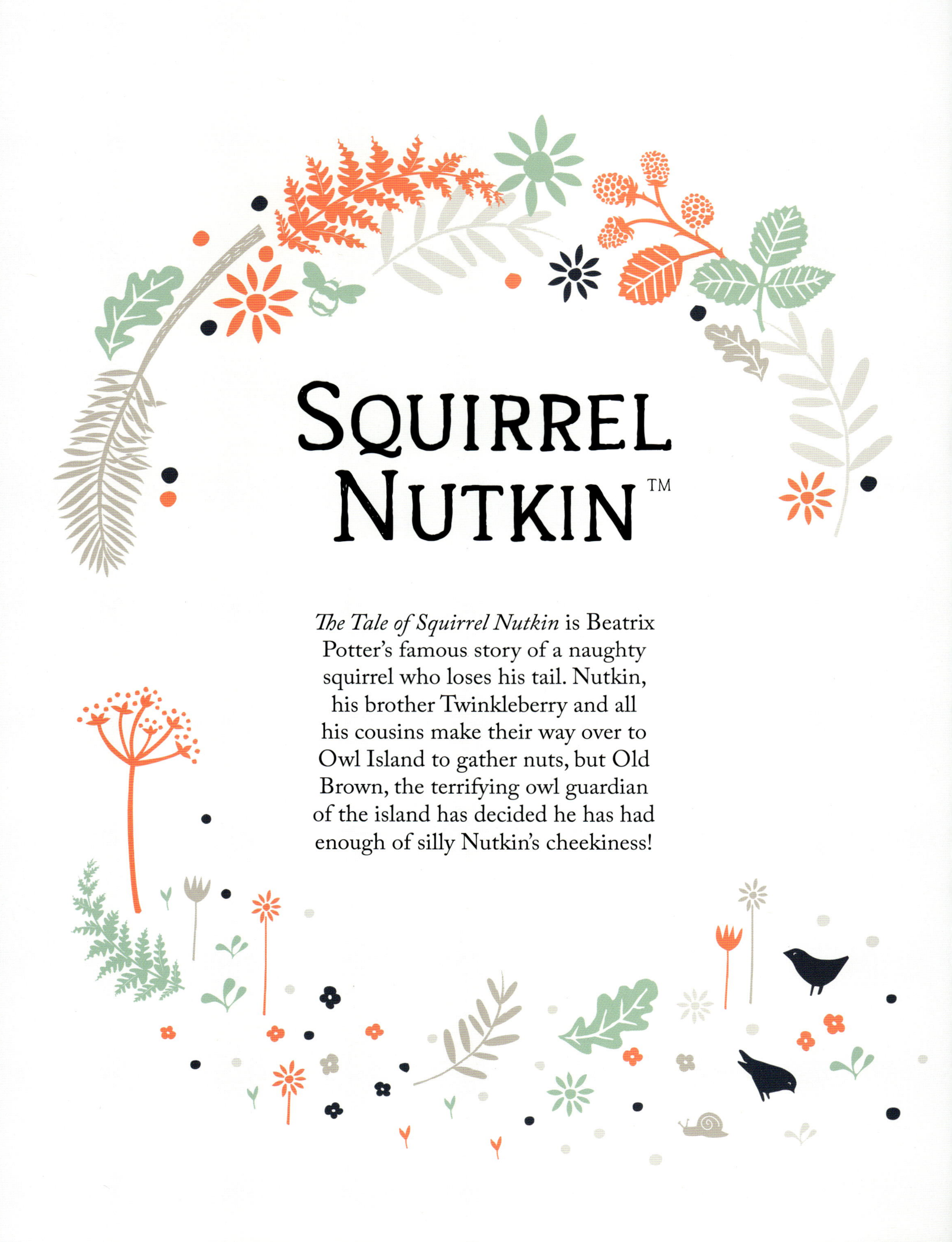

SQUIRREL NUTKIN™

The Tale of Squirrel Nutkin is Beatrix Potter's famous story of a naughty squirrel who loses his tail. Nutkin, his brother Twinkleberry and all his cousins make their way over to Owl Island to gather nuts, but Old Brown, the terrifying owl guardian of the island has decided he has had enough of silly Nutkin's cheekiness!

Materials

- 3mm (US C/2 or D/3) crochet hook
- 100% 8ply/DK cotton; colours used: burnt orange; nude; a small amount of brown and pale pink
- Stitch marker
- 8mm (⅓in) safety eyes
- Yarn needle
- Fibrefill stuffing

Finished size

13cm (5in) tall

Head

Round 1: Using burnt orange, 6 sc in a magic ring.

Round 2: 2 sc in each st. (12 sts)

Round 3: [1 sc, 2 sc in next st] to end. (18 sts)

Round 4: 1 sc, 2 sc in next st [2 sc, 2 sc in next st] 5 times, 1 sc. (24 sts)

Round 5: [3 sc, 2 sc in next st] to end. (30 sts)

Rounds 6–10: 1 sc in each st.

Round 11: 2 sc, 2 sc in next st, [4 sc, 2 sc in next st] 5 times, 2 sc. (36 sts)

Rounds 12 and 13: 1 sc in each st.

Round 14: 12 sc, [2 sc in next st, 1 sc] 5 times, 2 sc in next st, 13 sc. (42 sts)

Round 15: 1 sc in each st.

On the next few rounds we will do several colour changes. Remember to join the new colour in the last step of the previous st.

Round 16: 16 sc, change to nude, 11 sc, change to burnt orange, 15 sc.

Round 17: 14 sc, change to nude, 15 sc, change to burnt orange, 13 sc.

Round 18: [5 sc, sc2tog] twice, 1 sc, change to nude, 4 sc, sc2tog, 5 sc, sc2tog, 1 sc, change to burnt orange, 4 sc, sc2tog, 5 sc, sc2tog. (36 sts)

Round 19: 2 sc, [sc2tog, 4 sc] twice, change to nude, sc2tog, 4 sc, sc2tog, 3 sc, change to burnt orange, 1 sc, sc2tog, 4 sc, sc2tog, 2 sc. (30 sts)

Place safety eyes between Rounds 14 and 15 with 8 sts between them. Embroider cheeks using pale pink, and the nose using brown, following the pictures as a guide **(1)**.

Round 20: [3 sc, sc2tog] twice, 2 sc, change to nude, 1 sc, sc2tog, 3 sc, sc2tog, 1 sc, change to burnt orange, 2 sc, sc2tog, 3 sc, sc2tog. (24 sts)

Start stuffing the head at this point.

Round 21: 1 sc, sc2tog, 2 sc, sc2tog, 3 sc, change to nude, sc2tog, 2 sc, sc2tog, 1 sc, change to burnt orange, 1 sc, sc2tog, 2 sc, sc2tog. (18 sts)

Round 22: [1 sc, sc2tog] to end. (12 sts)

Round 23: [Sc2tog] 6 times. (6 sts)

Fasten off and close remaining sts through the front loops (see Techniques: Closing Remaining Stitches Through the Front Loops). Weave in ends (see Techniques: Hiding Ends Inside the Toy).

Body

Round 1: Using burnt orange, 6 sc in a magic ring.

Round 2: 2 sc in each st. (12 sts)

Round 3: 2 sc in each st. (24 sts)

Round 4: [3 sc, 2 sc in next st] to end. (30 sts)

Round 5: 2 sc, 2 sc in next st, [4 sc, 2 sc in next st] 5 times, 2 sc. (36 sts)

Rounds 6–8: 1 sc in each st.

Round 9: 2 sc, sc2tog, [4 sc, sc2tog] 5 times, 2 sc. (30 sts)

On the next few rounds we will do several colour changes. Remember to join the new colour in the last step of the previous st.

Round 10: 13 sc, change to nude, 4 sc, change to burnt orange, 13 sc.

Round 11: 11 sc, change to nude, 8 sc, change to burnt orange, 11 sc.

Round 12: [3 sc, sc2tog] twice, 1 sc, change to nude, 3 sc, sc2tog, 3 sc, change to burnt orange, sc2tog, 2 sc, sc2tog, 3 sc, sc2tog. (24 sts)

Start stuffing the body at this point.

Rounds 13 and 14: 9 sc, change to nude, 7 sc, change to burnt orange, 8 sc.

Round 15: [2 sc, sc2tog] twice, 1 sc, change to nude, 1 sc, sc2tog, 2 sc, sc2tog, change to burnt orange, [2 sc, sc2tog] twice. (18 sts)

Round 16: 7 sc, change to nude, 5 sc, change to burnt orange, 6 sc.

Round 17: 4 sc, sc2tog, 1 sc, change to nude, 5 sc, change to burnt orange, 1 sc, sc2tog, 3 sc. (16 sts)

Fasten off, leaving a long tail for sewing to the head.

Arms (make two)

Round 1: Using burnt orange, ch 2, 4 sc in the second ch from hook. (4 sts)

Round 2: 2 sc in each st. (8 sts)

Rounds 3–8: 1 sc in each st.

There is no need to stuff the arms.

Press the opening together with your fingers, with 4 sts on each side and join edges by working 1 sc into each pair of sts (see Techniques: Closing Limbs and Ears).

Fasten off, leaving a long tail for sewing to the body.

Ears (make two)

Round 1: Using burnt orange, 6 sc in a magic ring.

Round 2: 1 sc in each st.

Round 3: 2 sc in each st. (12 sts)

Round 4: 1 sc in each st.

On the next few rounds we will do several colour changes. Remember to join the new colour in the last step of the previous st.

Round 5: 1 sc, change to nude, 2 sc in next st, 1 sc, change to burnt orange, 2 sc in next st, [1 sc, 2 sc in next st] 4 times. (18 sts)

Rounds 6 and 7: 1 sc, change to nude, 4 sc, change to burnt orange, 13 sc.

Round 8: 1 sc, change to nude, sc2tog, 2 sc, change to burnt orange, [sc2tog] twice, [1 sc, sc2tog] 3 times. (12 sts)

Round 9: 1 sc, change to nude, 3 sc, change to burnt orange, 8 sc.

Press the opening together with your fingers, with 6 sts on each side and join edges by working 1 sc into each pair of sts.

Fasten off, leaving a long tail for sewing to the head **(2)**.

Tip

After sewing the tail, secure it with a few stitches to the back of your squirrel so it doesn't fall backwards.

Feet (make two)

Round 1: Using burnt orange, ch 2, 4 sc in the second ch from hook. (4 sts)

Round 2: 2 sc in each st. (8 sts)

Round 3: 1 sc in each st.

There is no need to stuff the feet.

Press the opening together with your fingers, with 4 sts on each side and join edges by working 1 sc into each pair of sts.

Fasten off, leaving a long tail for sewing to the body.

Tail

Round 1: Using nude, 6 sc in a magic ring.

Round 2: 2 sc BLO in each st. (12 sts)

Round 3: [1 sc, 2 sc in next st] to end. (18 sts)

Round 4: 1 sc BLO, 2 sc BLO in next st [2 sc BLO, 2 sc BLO in next st] 5 times, 1 sc BLO. (24 sts)

Round 5: [3 sc, 2 sc in next st] to end. (30 sts)

Round 6: 1 sc BLO in each st.

Round 7: 1 sc in each st.

Rounds 8 and 9: Rep Rounds 6 and 7 once more.

Round 10: Change to burnt orange, 1 sc BLO in each st.

Round 11: [3 sc, sc2tog] to end. (24 sts)

Round 12: 1 sc BLO in each st.

Round 13: 1 sc in each st.

Rounds 14 and 15: Rep Rounds 12 and 13 once more.

Round 16: 1 sc BLO in each st.

Round 17: 1 sc, sc2tog, [2 sc, sc2tog] 5 times, 1 sc. (18 sts)

Round 18: 1 sc BLO in each st.

Round 19: 1 sc in each st.

Round 20: 1 sc BLO in each st.

Round 21: [1 sc, sc2tog] to end. (12 sts)

Round 22: 1 sc BLO in each st.

Round 23: 1 sc in each st.

Round 24: 1 sc BLO in each st.

Round 25: 1 sc. Leave remaining sts unworked.

Press the opening together with your fingers, with 6 sts on each side and join edges by working 1 sc into each pair of sts.

Fasten off, leaving a long tail for sewing to the back of the body.

You'll see that the tail presents a spiral of remaining front loops. Join nude in the first front loop above the magic ring on Round 1, 1 slst in next st, [ch 4 **(3)**, 1 slst in next st] in all remaining nude front loops.

Fasten off and weave in ends (see Techniques: Weaving in Ends).

Now join burnt orange in the first front loop of Round 12, 1 slst in next st, [ch 4, 1 slst in next st] in all remaining burnt orange front loops. Fasten off and weave in ends.

Assembly

Pin the head to the body and sew in place (see Techniques: Attaching Heads). When sewing through the nude part of the neck, work the needle through the back loops of the stitches, so the burnt orange yarn doesn't show.

Sew the arms to the sides of the body between Rounds 15 and 16 of the body.

Curve the ears and sew them to the head between Rounds 4 and 5, counted from the magic ring on Round 1.

Sew the feet to the base of the body between Rounds 4 and 5 **(4)**.

Sew the tail to the back of the body between Rounds 6 and 7. So that the tail doesn't fall backwards, secure the tail to the back of the body with some extra stitches.

Weave in all ends inside the body.

Old Brown Owl™

Old Brown allows the squirrels to gather nuts on his island in return for gifts including three dead mice, a mole, seven minnows, six beetles and some honey. But rather than gathering nuts peacefully like the rest of his family, Squirrel Nutkin taunts Old Brown with silly dances and annoying riddles.

Materials

- 3mm (US C/2 or D/3) crochet hook
- 100% 8ply/DK cotton; colours used: beige; light brown; brown; a small amount of pale pink
- Stitch marker
- 8mm (⅓in) safety eyes
- Yarn needle
- Fibrefill stuffing

Finished size

16cm (6¼in) tall

Base of body

Round 1: Using beige, 6 sc in a magic ring.

Round 2: 2 sc in each st. (12 sts)

Round 3: 2 sc in each st. (24 sts)

Round 4: [3 sc, 2 sc in next st] to end. (30 sts)

Round 5: 2 sc, 2 sc in next st, [4 sc, 2 sc in next st] 5 times, 2 sc. (36 sts)

Round 6: [5 sc, 2 sc in next st] to end. (42 sts)

Round 7: [20 sc, 2 sc in next st] twice. (44 sts)

Fasten off and weave in ends (see Techniques: Weaving in Ends). Set aside.

Head

Round 1: Using light brown, 6 sc in a magic ring.

Round 2: 2 sc in each st. (12 sts)

Round 3: 2 sc in each st. (24 sts)

Round 4: [3 sc, 2 sc in next st] to end. (30 sts)

Round 5: 2 sc, 2 sc in next st, [4 sc, 2 sc in next st] 5 times, 2 sc. (36 sts)

Round 6: [5 sc, 2 sc in the next s] to end. (42 sts)

Round 7: 3 sc, 2 sc in next st, [6 sc, 2 sc in next st] 5 times, 3 sc. (48 sts)

Round 8: [7 sc, 2 sc in next st] to end. (54 sts)

Round 9: 4 sc, 2 sc in next st, [8 sc, 2 sc in next st] 5 times, 4 sc. (60 sts)

Rounds 10–14: 1 sc in each st.

On the next few rounds we will change colour several times. Remember to join the new colour in the last step of the previous st.

Round 15: 23 sc, change to beige, 4 sc, change to light brown, 7 sc, change to beige, 4 sc, change to light brown, 22 sc.

Round 16: 22 sc, change to beige, 6 sc, change to light brown, 5 sc, change to beige, 6 sc, change to light brown, 21 sc.

Round 17: 21 sc, change to beige, 8 sc, change to light brown, 3 sc, change to beige, 8 sc, change to light brown, 20 sc.

Rounds 18–23: 20 sc, change to beige, 10 sc, change to light brown, 1 sc, change to beige, 10 sc, change to light brown, 19 sc.

Round 24: 21 sc, change to beige, 8 sc, change to light brown, 3 sc, change to beige, 8 sc, change to light brown, 20 sc.

Round 25: 22 sc, change to beige, 6 sc, change to light brown, 5 sc, change to beige, 6 sc, change to light brown, 21 sc.

Round 26: 23 sc, change to beige, 4 sc, change to light brown, 7 sc, change to beige, 4 sc, change to light brown, 22 sc.

Round 27: 4 sc, sc2tog, [8 sc, sc2tog] 5 times, 4 sc. (54 sts)

Place safety eyes between Rounds 22 and 23 into the beige spots with 9 sts between them and embroider a straight brown line above them. Embroider the cheeks using pale pink, following the pictures as a guide **(3)**.

Round 28: 1 sc in each st.

Round 29: 1 sc FLO in each st.

Round 30: [ch 4, 1 sc in the second ch from hook, 1 sc in each ch to end, 3 slst] to end.

Fasten off and weave in ends.

Body

Turn the head upside down and join beige in one of the back loops of Round 29, at the back of the head **(1)**.

Round 1: 1 sc BLO in each st of Round 29. (54 sts)

Rounds 2–5: 1 sc in each st.

Round 6: [7 sc, sc2tog] to end. (48 sts)

Rounds 7–12: 1 sc in each st.

Round 13: [10 sc, sc2tog] to end. (44 sts)

Rounds 14 and 15: 1 sc in each st.

Stuff the body firmly. Place the base on top of the opening of the body, like a lid (wrong side down).

Round 16: 1 sc in each st, working through each st of the base and the body at the same time **(2)**. Before completely closing both pieces together, add some extra stuffing.

Round 17: 1 sc in each st.

Fasten off invisibly (see Fastening off Invisibly) and weave in ends (see Techniques: Hiding Ends Inside the Toy).

Beak

Round 1: Using brown, 6 sc in a magic ring.

Round 2: 2 sc in each st. (12 sts)

Rounds 3 and 4: 1 sc in each st.

Fasten off, leaving a long tail for sewing to the head.

Wings (make two)

Round 1: Using light brown, 6 sc in a magic ring.

Round 2: 2 sc in each st. (12 sts)

Rounds 3–5: 1 sc in each st.

Round 6: [1 sc, 2 sc in next st] to end. (18 sts)

Round 7: 1 sc in each st.

Round 8: Change to beige, 1 sc in each st.

Round 9: 1 sc in each st.

There is no need to stuff the wings.

Round 10: 1 sc, 2 sc in next st, [2 sc, 2 sc in next st] 5 times, 1 sc. (24 sts)

Rounds 11–14: 1 sc in each st.

Press the opening together with your fingers, with 12 sts on each side and join edges by working 1 sc into each pair of sts (see Techniques: Closing Limbs and Ears).

Fasten off, leaving a long tail to sew to the body **(4)**.

Assembly

Stuff the beak slightly and sew it between the eyes **(5)**.

Sew the wings to the sides of the body between Rounds 2 and 3.

Using light brown, embroider straight short lines on the chest of Old brown, as if they were small feathers.

Weave in all ends inside the body.

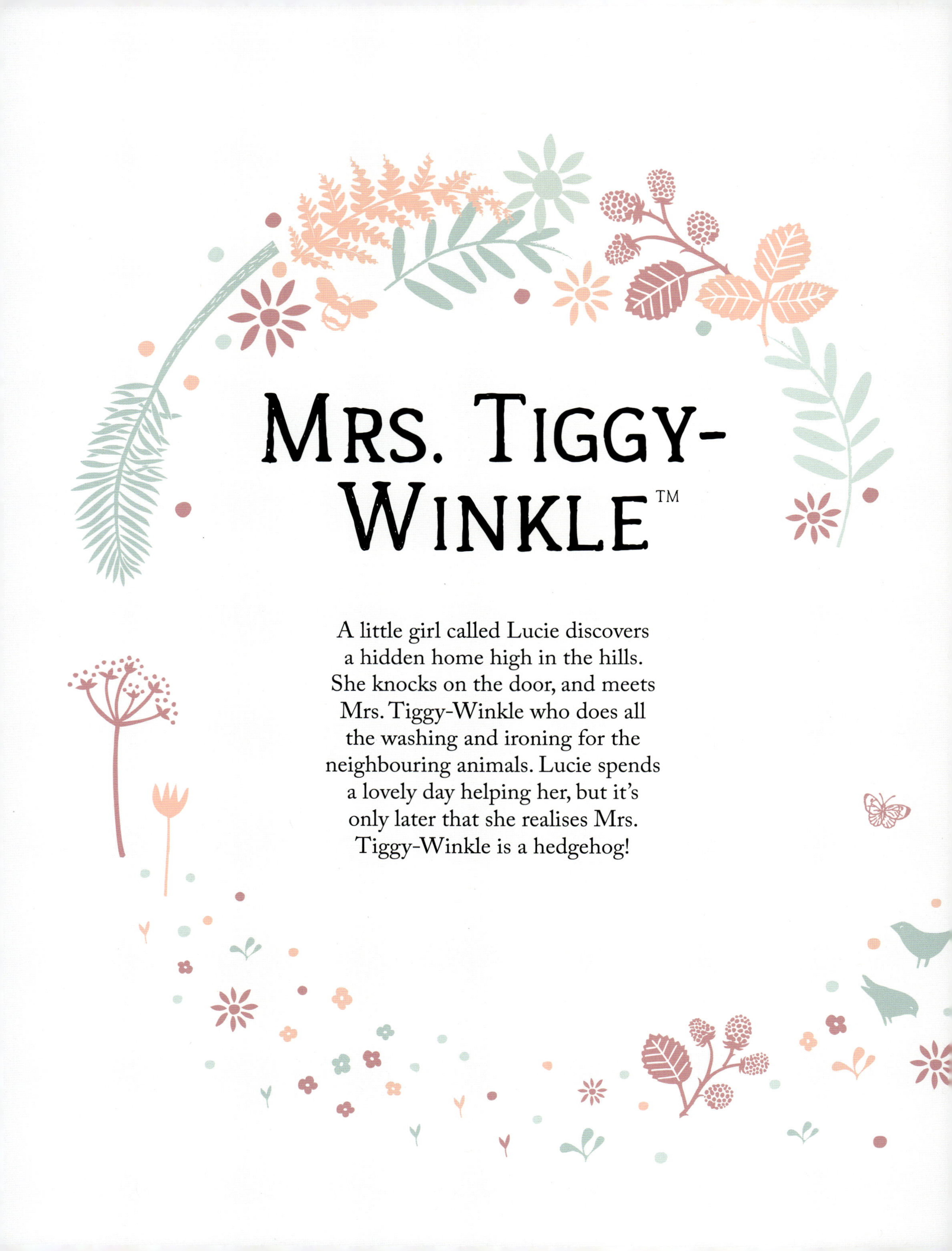

Mrs. Tiggy-Winkle™

A little girl called Lucie discovers
a hidden home high in the hills.
She knocks on the door, and meets
Mrs. Tiggy-Winkle who does all
the washing and ironing for the
neighbouring animals. Lucie spends
a lovely day helping her, but it's
only later that she realises Mrs.
Tiggy-Winkle is a hedgehog!

Materials

- 3mm (US C/2 or D/3) crochet hook
- 100% 8ply/DK cotton; colours used: beige; light brown; curry yellow; pale pink; white; mustard; a small amount of black
- Stitch marker
- 8mm (⅓in) safety eyes
- Yarn needle
- Fibrefill stuffing

Finished size

17cm (6¾in) tall

Snout

Round 1: Using beige, 6 sc in a magic ring.

Round 2: 1 sc in each st.

Round 3: 2 sc in the next 3 sts, 3 sc. (9 sts)

Round 4: 2 sc in the next 4 sts, 5 sc. (13 sts)

Round 5: 1 sc in each st.

Fasten off, leaving a long tail for sewing to the body. Set aside.

Base of body

Round 1: Using light brown, 6 sc in a magic ring.

Round 2: 2 sc in each st. (12 sts)

Round 3: 2 sc in each st. (24 sts)

Round 4: [3 sc, 2 sc in next st] to end. (30 sts)

Round 5: 2 sc, 2 sc in next st, [4 sc, 2 sc in next st] 5 times, 2 sc. (36 sts)

Round 6: [5 sc, 2 sc in next st] to end. (42 sts)

Round 7: 3 sc, 2 sc in next st, [6 sc, 2 sc in next st] 5 times, 3 sc. (48 sts)

Round 8: 1 sc in each st.

Fasten off invisibly (see Techniques: Fastening off Invisibly) and weave in ends (see Techniques: Weaving in Ends). Set aside.

Body with petticoat

Using curry yellow for the petticoat, ch 48, 1 sc in the 48th ch from hook to form a ring, making sure not to twist the chain.

Round 1: 1 sc in each ch to end. (48 sts)

Rounds 2–4: 1 sc in each st.

Now take the base and place it over your ring like a lid, wrong side up.

Round 5: 1 sc in each st, working through each st of the petticoat and each st of the base at the same time **(1)**. (48 sts)

Rounds 6–13: 1 sc in each st.

Round 14: Change to pale pink for the dress, 1 sc in each st.

Round 15: 1 sc BLO in each st.

Start stuffing the body at this point.

Rounds 16 and 17: 1 sc in each st.

Round 18: 3 sc, sc2tog, [6 sc, sc2tog] 5 times, 3 sc. (42 sts)

Round 19: [5 sc, sc2tog] to end. (36 sts)

Round 20: 2 sc, sc2tog, [4 sc, sc2tog] 5 times, 2 sc. (30 sts)

Round 21: Change to beige for the head, 1 sc in each st.

Round 22: 2 sc in each st. (60 sts)

Stuff the neck area firmly.

Rounds 23–37: 1 sc in each st.

Place safety eyes between Rounds 26 and 27, with 10 sts between them. Embroider cheeks using pale pink **(2)**.

Round 38: 4 sc, sc2tog, [8 sc, sc2tog] 5 times, 4 sc. (54 sts)

Round 39: [7 sc, sc2tog] to end. (48 sts)

Round 40: 3 sc, sc2tog, [6 sc, sc2tog] 5 times, 3 sc. (42 sts)

Round 41: [5 sc, sc2tog] to end. (36 sts)

Start stuffing the head at this point.

Round 42: 2 sc, sc2tog, [4 sc, sc2tog] 5 times, 2 sc. (30 sts)

Round 43: [3 sc, sc2tog] to end. (24 sts)

Round 44: 1 sc, sc2tog, [2 sc, sc2tog] 5 times, 1 sc. (18 sts)

Stuff firmly.

Round 45: [1 sc, sc2tog] to end. (12 sts)

Round 46: [Sc2tog] 6 times. (6 sts)

Fasten off and close remaining sts through the front loops (see Techniques: Closing Remaining Stitches Through the Front Loops). Weave in ends (see Techniques: Hiding Ends Inside the Toy).

Skirt

Turn the body upside down and join pale pink in the first remaining front loop of Round 15, at the back of the body.

Round 1: 1 sc FLO in each st of Round 15. (48 sts)

Round 2: [7 sc, 2 sc in next st] to end. (54 sts)

Round 3: 4 sc, 2 sc in next st, [8 sc, 2 sc in next st] 5 times, 4 sc. (60 sts)

Rounds 4–15: 1 sc in each st.

Fasten off invisibly and weave in ends.

Ears (make two)

Round 1: Using beige, ch 2, 4 sc in the second ch from hook. (4 sts)

Round 2: 2 sc in each st. (8 sts)

Round 3: 1 sc in each st.

There is no need to stuff the ears.

Round 4: Press the opening together with your fingers with 4 sts on each side and join edges by working 1 sc into each pair of sts (see Techniques: Closing Limbs and Ears).

Fasten off, leaving a long tail for sewing to the head.

Tip

The skirt must cover the petticoat. Crochet an extra round or two if necessary.

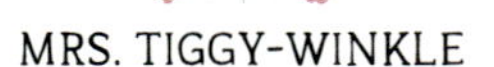

TIP

Use your fingers to stretch the hedgehog spikes so they don't curl up.

HAIR WITH SPIKES

Round 1: Using light brown, 6 sc in a magic ring.

Round 2: 2 sc in each st. (12 sts)

Round 3: [1 sc, 2 sc in next st] to end. (18 sts)

Round 4: 1 sc, 2 sc in next st, [2 sc, 2 sc in next st] 5 times, 1 sc. (24 sts)

Round 5: [3 sc, 2 sc in next st] to end. (30 sts)

Round 6: 2 sc, 2 sc in next st, [4 sc, 2 sc in next st] 5 times, 2 sc. (36 sts)

Round 7: [5 sc, 2 sc in next st] to end. (42 sts)

Round 8: 3 sc, 2 sc in next st, [6 sc, 2 sc in next st] 5 times, 3 sc. (48 sts)

Round 9: [7 sc, 2 sc in next st] to end. (54 sts)

Round 10: 4 sc, 2 sc in next st, [8 sc, 2 sc in next st] 5 times, 4 sc. (60 sts)

Round 11: [29 sc, 2 sc in next st] twice. (62 sts)

Rounds 12–20: 1 sc in each st.

Round 21: 1 sc BLO in each st.

Round 22: [Ch 4, 1 slst in second ch from hook, 1 slst in each ch (3 sts), 2 sc] to end. (31 spikes)

Fasten off, leaving a long tail for sewing to the head.

SECOND ROUND OF SPIKES

Now join light brown in the first front loops of Round 21 of the hair **(3)**.

Round 1: 1 sc, [ch 4, 1 slst in second ch from hook, 1 slst in each ch (3 sts), 2 sc] 30 times, ch 4, 1 slst in second ch from hook, 1 slst in each st along ch (3 sts), 1 sc. (31 spikes)

Fasten off and weave in ends.

CAP

Round 1: Using white, 6 sc in a magic ring.

Round 2: 2 sc in each st. (12 sts)

Round 3: 2 sc in each st. (24 sts)

Round 4: [1 sc, 2 sc in next st] to end. (36 sts)

Round 5: [5 sc, 2 sc in next st] to end. (42 sts)

Round 6: 3 sc, 2 sc in next st, [6 sc, 2 sc in next st] 5 times, 3 sc. (48 sts)

Round 7: [7 sc, 2 sc in next st] to end. (54 sts)

Round 8: 4 sc, 2 sc in next st, [8 sc, 2 sc in next st] 5 times, 4 sc. (60 sts)

Round 9: [9 sc, 2 sc in next st] to end. (66 sts)

Rounds 10–18: 1 sc in each st.

Round 19: 36 sc BLO, 30 sc.

Round 20: 3 sc in each of next 36 sts. Leave remaining sts unworked. (108 sts)

Row 21: Ch 1 (does not count as a st), turn, 1 sc in each of next 108 sts.

Fasten off, leaving a long tail for sewing to the head **(4)**.

ARMS (make two)

Round 1: Using beige, 5 sc in a magic ring.

Round 2: 2 sc in each st. (10 sts)

Rounds 3–5: 1 sc in each st.

Round 6: Change to pale pink, 1 sc BLO in each st.

Rounds 7–13: 1 sc in each st.

There is no need to stuff the arms.

Press the opening together with your fingers with 5 sts on each side and join edges by working 1 sc into each pair of sts.

Fasten off, leaving a long tail for sewing to the body.

Apron

The apron is worked in rows using white.

Row 1: Leaving a long initial tail, ch 14, 1 hdc in the third ch from hook, 5 hdc, 6 sc, ch 1, turn. (12 sts)

Row 2: 6 sc BLO, 6 hdc BLO, ch 1, turn.

Row 3: Ch 1, 6 hdc BLO, 6 sc BLO, ch 1, turn.

Rows 4–15: Rep Rows 2 and 3 another 6 times.

Before fastening off, ch 40 to create the first strap.

Fasten off, leaving a long tail for tying around the neck.

Ch 40, fasten off and sew to other end of apron, opposite first strap **(5)**.

Basket

Round 1: Using mustard, 6 sc in a magic ring.

Round 2: 2 sc in each st. (12 sts)

Round 3: 2 sc in each st. (24 sts)

Round 4: [3 sc, 2 sc in next st] to end. (30 sts)

Round 5: 2 sc, 2 sc in next st, [4 sc, 2 sc in next st] 5 times, 2 sc. (36 sts)

Round 6: [11 sc, 2 sc in next st] to end. (39 sts)

Round 7: 1 sc BLO in each st.

Important: From now on, use traditional v-shaped sc stitches.

Round 8: [1 sc BLO, 1 sc] to last st, 1 sc BLO.

Round 9: [1 spike st (see Crochet Stitches: Special Stitches), 1 sc BLO] to last st, 1 spike st.

Rounds 10–13: Rep Rounds 8 and 9 twice more.

Fasten off invisibly (see Fastening off Invisibly) and weave in ends.

Handles (make two)

Using mustard, and leaving a long initial tail, ch 10.

Fasten off, leaving a long tail for sewing to the edge of the basket **(6)**.

White Sheet

The sheet is worked in rows using white.

Row 1: Ch 18, 1 hdc in the third ch from hook, 1 hdc in each ch to end. (16 sts).

Rows 2–10: Ch 1, turn, 1 hdc in each st.

Fasten off and weave in ends **(7)**.

Assembly

Sew the snout to the body between the eyes, starting between Rounds 28 and 29. Using black, embroider the nose on the tip of the snout following the pictures as a guide.

Sew the arms to the sides of the body between Rounds 19 and 20.

Sew the hair spikes to the head and arrange the spikes with your fingers.

Sew the little ears to the hair between the rounds of spikes, in line with the eyes.

Sew the cap to the head, with the ruffle over the forehead.

Tie the apron around the waist, right above where the skirt begins.

Weave in all ends inside the body.

Lift the back of the skirt up to make the petticoat visible.

Sew the handles to the basket, one opposite the other, leaving 5 sts between the ends of each handle.

Weave in all ends.

5

6

7

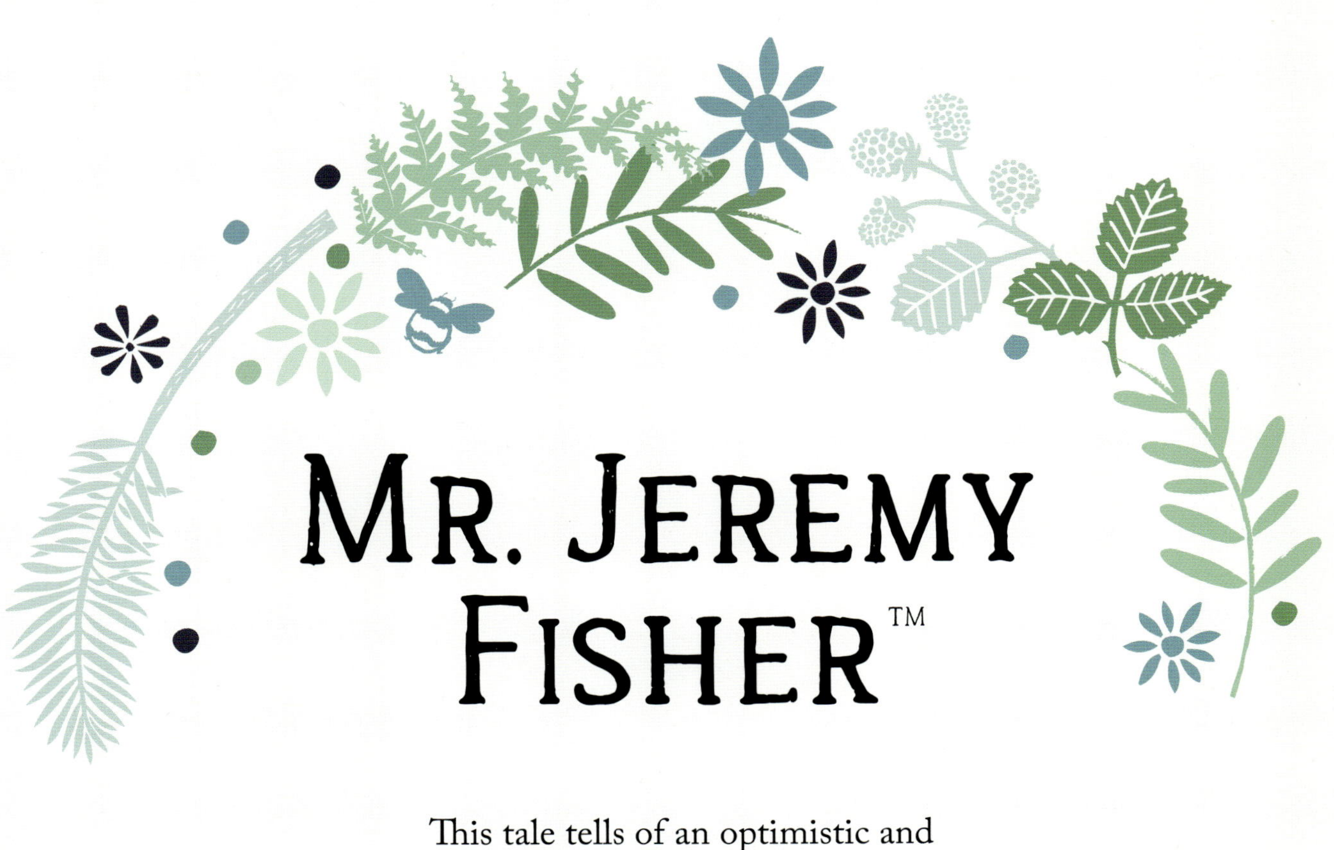

Mr. Jeremy Fisher™

This tale tells of an optimistic and slightly accident-prone frog, who sets off on a fishing expedition across the pond, only to find himself bitten on the toe by a water-beetle, fighting with a stickleback, and eventually nearly eaten by a trout!

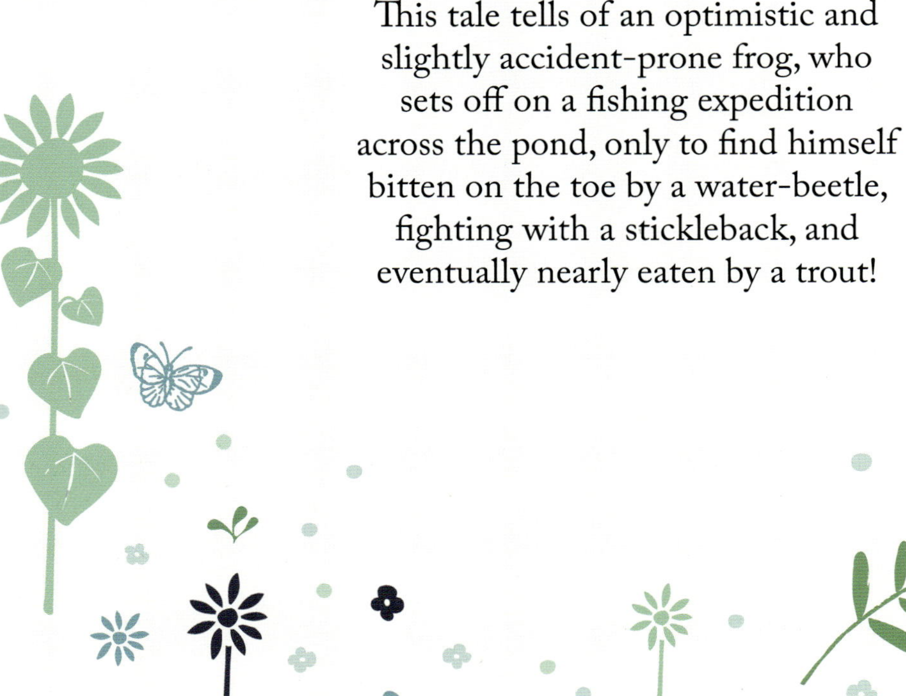

Materials

- 2.5mm (US B/1 or C/2) crochet hook
- 100% 4ply/fingering cotton; colours used: black; white; curry yellow; olive; pale pink; dark rose
- Stitch marker
- 8mm (⅓in) safety eyes
- Yarn needle
- Fibrefill stuffing

Finished size

13cm (5in) tall

Leg 1

Round 1: Using black for the galoshes, ch 6, 2 sc in the second ch from hook, 3 sc, 4 sc in next st (this will allow you to work on the other side of the chain), 3 sc, 2 sc in the last st. (14 sts)

Round 2: 1 sc in each st.

Round 3: 5 sc, sc2tog, 1 sc, sc2tog, 4 sc. (12 sts)

Round 4: Change to white for the socks, 4 sc, [sc2tog] twice, 4 sc. (10 sts)

Round 5: 3 sc, [sc2tog] twice, 3 sc. (8 sts)

Round 6: 1 sc in each st.

Stuff the feet firmly.

Round 7: Change to curry yellow, 1 sc BLO in each st.

Round 8: 1 sc in each st.

Round 9: Change to olive, 1 sc in each st.

Round 10: 1 sc in each st.

Start stuffing the leg and continue doing so as you work.

Round 11: Change to curry yellow, 1 sc in each st.

Round 12: 1 sc in each st.

Round 13: Change to olive, 1 sc in each st.

Round 14: 1 sc in each st.

Rounds 15–18: Rep Rounds 11–14 once more.

Round 19: Change to curry yellow, 1 sc in each st.

Round 20: 1 sc in each st.

Round 21: Change to olive, 1 sc in each st.

Round 22: 5 sc. Leave remaining sts unworked.

Fasten off invisibly (see Techniques: Fastening off Invisibly) and weave in ends (see Techniques: Weaving in Ends). Set aside.

Leg 2

Work as for leg 1 but do not fasten off at the end. Continue with the body.

Body and Head

Round 23: With leg 2 still on your hook, ch 6 and join to leg 1 with a sc **(1)** (see Techniques: Joining Legs), pm here for new beg of round (IMPORTANT: make sure both feet point away from you), 7 sc around leg 1, 1 sc into each ch of 6-ch, 8 sc around leg 2, 1 sc into other side of each ch of 6-ch. (28 sts)

Round 24: [13 sc, 2 sc in next st] to end. (30 sts)

Round 25: [2 sc, 2 sc in next st] to end. (40 sts)

Round 26: Change to pale pink, 1 sc BLO in each st.

Rounds 27–33: 1 sc in each st.

Start stuffing the body.

Round 34: [8 sc, sc2tog] to end. (36 sts)

On the next few rounds we will change colour several times. Remember to join the new colour in the last step of the previous st.

Round 35: 14 sc, change to white, 2 sc, change to pale pink, 20 sc.

Round 36: 13 sc, change to white, 4 sc, change to pale pink, 19 sc.

Round 37: 12 sc, change to white, 6 sc, change to pale pink, 18 sc.

Round 38: 11 sc, change to white, 8 sc, change to pale pink, 17 sc.

Round 39: 10 sc, change to white, 10 sc, change to pale pink, 16 sc.

You should have a white triangle at the front centre of his chest.

Round 40: Change to olive, 1 sc BLO in each st. (36 sts)

Round 41: 13 sc, 2 hdc FLO in each of the next 6 sts, 17 sc. (42 sts)

Rounds 42–44: 1 sc in each st.

Round 45: [5 sc, sc2tog] to end. (36 sts)

Round 46: 2 sc, sc2tog, [4 sc, sc2tog], 2 sc. (30 sts)

Place safety eyes between Rounds 43 and 44, to the sides of the protuberance. Embroider cheeks using pale pink. The eyes are quite big, so use your hook to make a hole, enlarge it a bit and then place the eyes.

Start stuffing the head at this point.

Round 47: [3 sc, sc2tog] to end. (24 sts)

Round 48: 1 sc, sc2tog, [2 sc, sc2tog] 5 times, 1 sc. (18 sts)

Stuff firmly.

Round 49: [1 sc, sc2tog] to end. (12 sts)

Round 50: [Sc2tog] 6 times. (6 sts)

Fasten off and close remaining sts through the front loops (see Techniques: Closing Remaining Stitches Through the Front Loops). Weave in ends (see Techniques: Hiding Ends Inside the Toy).

Tip

Remember that when joining the legs with the chain, you should see the back of them and the galoshes should be pointing forward.

ARMS (make two)

Round 1: Using olive, ch 2, 4 sc in the second ch from hook. (4 sts)

Round 2: 2 sc in each st. (8 sts)

Rounds 3–5: 1 sc in each st.

Round 6: Change to dark rose, 1 sc BLO in each st.

There is no need to stuff the arms.

Rounds 7–16: 1 sc in each st.

Press the opening together with your fingers, with 4 sts on each side and join edges by working 1 sc into each pair of sts (see Techniques: Closing Limbs and Ears).

Fasten off, leaving a long tail for sewing to the body.

COAT

The coat is actually a long vest, but when you put it on him it will look like a coat because of his olive and dark rose arms. The vest is worked in rows from the top down, using dark rose.

Row 1: Ch 25, 1 sc in the second ch from hook, 1 sc in each ch to end, ch 1, turn. (24 sts)

Row 2: 24 sc, ch 1, turn.

Row 3: 3 sc, ch 6, skip the following 4 sts (to create first armhole), 10 sc, ch 6, skip the following 4 sts (to create second armhole), 3 sc, ch 1, turn (see Techniques: Creating Armholes on Jackets).

Row 4: 3 sc, 1 sc in each ch of 6-ch, 10 sc, 1 sc in each ch of second 6-ch, 3 sc, ch 1, turn. (28 sts)

Rows 5–19: 1 sc in each st, ch 1, turn.

Row 20: 1 sc in each st.

Row 21: Ch 1, rotate the work 90 degrees clockwise and work 20 sc along the side of the vest, working into the spaces between rows. When you reach the top edge, work 24 sc in the remaining loops of the foundation chain, then ch 1, rotate the piece 90 degrees clockwise again and work 20 sc along the other side of the vest, working into the spaces between rows (see Techniques: Edging Flat Pieces).

Fasten off and weave in ends **(2)**.

ASSEMBLY

Using a bit of olive, embroider the eyelids as follows: using your yarn needle, make a straight st right above each eye. Working over and under the straight stitch, wrap your yarn around it to thicken it **(3)**.

Using curry yellow, embroider some spots above one of the eyes, following the pictures as a guide **(4)**.

Using a bit of pale pink, embroider two straight lines to mark the edges of the pink vest against the white shirt, following the pictures as a guide **(5)**.

Sew the arms to the sides of the body between Rounds 38 and 39, with 12 stitches between them on the back.

Slip his arms into the armholes of the coat.

Weave in all ends inside the body.

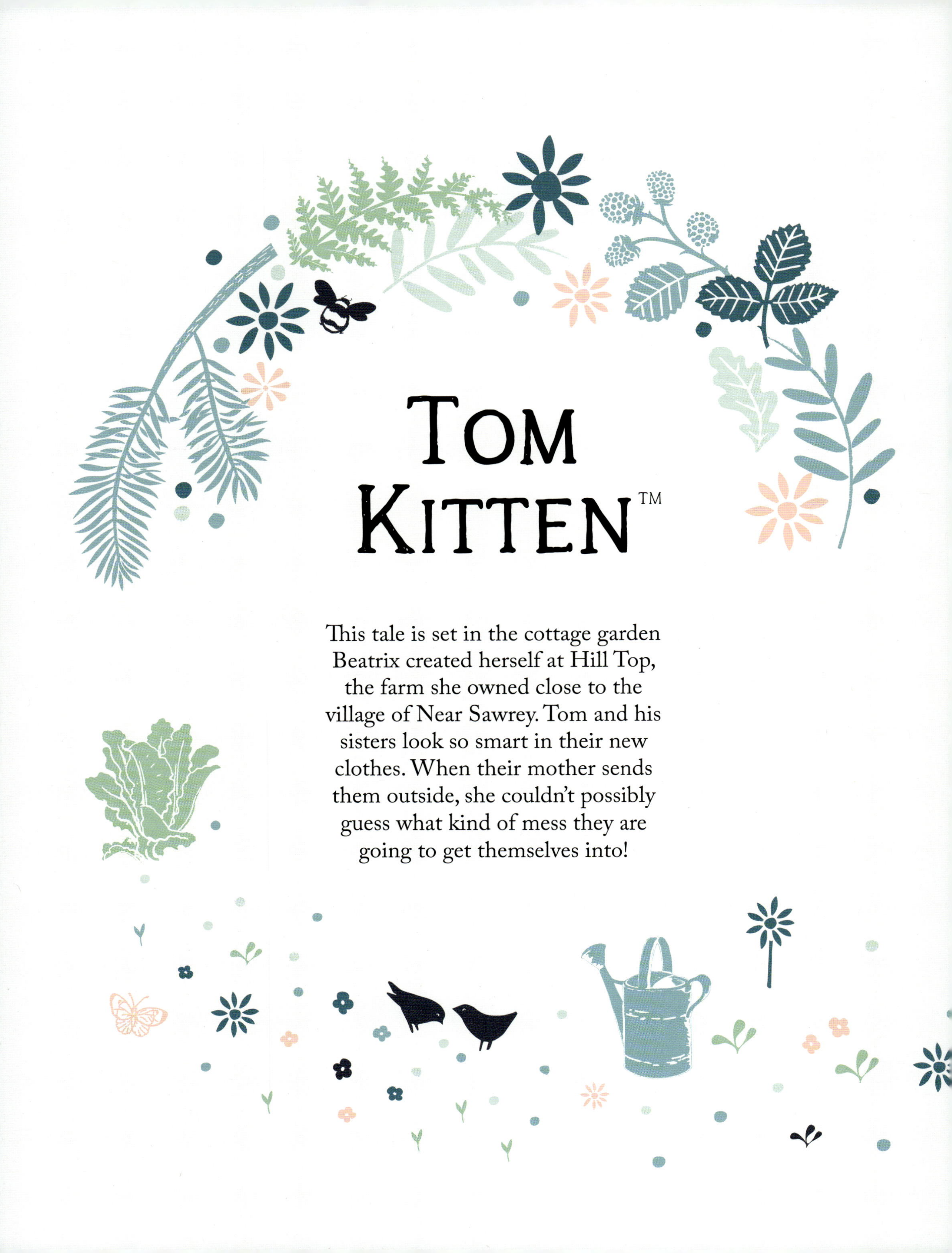

Tom Kitten™

This tale is set in the cottage garden Beatrix created herself at Hill Top, the farm she owned close to the village of Near Sawrey. Tom and his sisters look so smart in their new clothes. When their mother sends them outside, she couldn't possibly guess what kind of mess they are going to get themselves into!

MATERIALS

- 3mm (US C/2 or D/3) crochet hook
- 100% 8ply/DK cotton; colours used: dark brown; light brown; beige; light blue; a small amount of pale pink
- Stitch marker
- 8mm (⅓in) safety eyes
- Fibrefill stuffing
- Yarn needle

FINISHED SIZE

18cm (7in) tall

LEG 1

Round 1: Using dark brown, 6 sc in a magic ring. (6 sts)

Round 2: 2 sc in each st. (12 sts)

Round 3: [1 sc, 2 sc in next st] to end. (18 sts)

Round 4: Change to light brown, 1 sc in each st.

Round 5: 1 sc in each st.

Round 6: [4 sc, sc2tog] to end. (15 sts)

Rounds 7–11: 1 sc in each st.

Fasten off invisibly (see Techniques: Fastening off Invisibly) and weave in ends (see Techniques: Weaving in Ends). Set aside.

LEG 2

Work as for leg 1, but do not fasten off. Continue with the body.

BODY

Round 12: With leg 2 still on your hook, 4 sc, ch 3 and join to leg 1 with a sc **(1)** (see Techniques: Joining Legs), pm for new beg of round, 14 sc around leg 1, 1 sc into each ch of 3-ch, 15 sc around leg 2 and 1 sc into other side of each ch of 3-ch. (36 sts)

Rounds 13–17: 1 sc in each st.

Stuff the legs firmly. On the next few rounds we will change colour several times. Remember to join the new colour in the last step of the previous st.

Round 18: Change to dark brown, 11 sc, change to light brown, 4 sc, change to beige, 4 sc, change to light brown, 4 sc, change to dark brown, 13 sc.

Round 19: Change to light brown, 14 sc, change to beige, 7 sc, change to light brown, 15 sc.

Round 20: 13 sc, change to beige, 9 sc, change to light brown, 14 sc.

Round 21: Change to dark brown, 12 sc, change to light brown, 1 sc, change to beige, 9 sc, change to light brown, 1 sc, change to dark brown, 13 sc.

Round 22: Change to light brown, 2 sc, sc2tog, 4 sc, sc2tog, 3 sc, change to beige, 1 sc, sc2tog, 6 sc, change to light brown, sc2tog, 4 sc, sc2tog, 4 sc, sc2tog. (30 sts)

Start stuffing the body at this point.

Round 23: 11 sc, change to beige, 8 sc, change to light brown, 11 sc.

Round 24: Change to dark brown, 10 sc, change to light brown, 1 sc, change to beige, 8 sc, change to light brown, 1 sc, change to dark brown, 10 sc.

Round 25: Change to light brown, 11 sc, change to beige, 8 sc, change to light brown, 11 sc.

Round 26: 3 sc, sc2tog, 3 sc, sc2tog, 1 sc, change to beige, 2 sc, sc2tog, 4 sc, change to light brown, sc2tog, 3 sc, sc2tog, 2 sc, sc2tog. (24 sts)

Round 27: Change to dark brown, 8 sc, change to light brown, 1 sc, change to beige, 7 sc, change to light brown, 1 sc, change to dark brown, 7 sc. (24 sts)

Round 28: 9 sc, change to beige, 7 sc, change to light brown, 8 sc.

Stuff the neck area firmly.

Round 29: 1 sc, sc2tog, 2 sc, sc2tog, 2 sc, change to beige, sc2tog, 2 sc, sc2tog, 1 sc, change to light brown, 1 sc, sc2tog, 2 sc, sc2tog, 1 sc. (18 sts)

Fasten off, leaving a long tail for sewing to the head.

HEAD

Round 1: Using light brown, 6 sc in a magic ring.

Round 2: 2 sc in each st. (12 sts)

On the next few rounds we will change colour several times. Remember to join the new colour in the last step of the previous st.

Round 3: 2 sc in each of next 4 sts, change to beige, 2 sc in each of next 4 sts, change to light brown, 2 sc in each of last 4 sts. (24 sts)

Round 4: [1 sc, 2 sc in next st] 4 times, change to beige, [1 sc, 2 sc in next st] 4 times, change to light brown, [1 sc, 2 sc in next st] 4 times. (36 sts)

Round 5: [5 sc, 2 sc in next st] twice, change to beige, [5 sc, 2 sc in next st] twice, change to light brown, [5 sc, 2 sc in next st] twice. (42 sts)

Round 6: 3 sc, 2 sc in next st, 6 sc, 2 sc in next st, 3 sc, change to beige, 3 sc, 2 sc in next st, 6 sc, 2 sc in next st, 3 sc, change to light brown, 3 sc, 2 sc in next st, 6 sc, 2 sc in next st, 3 sc. (48 sts)

Round 7: [7 sc, 2 sc in next st] twice, change to beige, [7 sc, 2 sc in next st] twice, change to light brown, [7 sc, 2 sc in next st] twice. (54 sts)

Round 8: 20 sc, change to beige, 14 sc, change to light brown, 20 sc.

Round 9: 22 sc, change to beige, 10 sc, change to light brown, 22 sc.

Round 10: 24 sc, change to beige, 6 sc, change to light brown, 24 sc.

Round 11: 1 sc in each st.

Round 12: Change to dark brown, 20 sc, change to light brown, 15 sc, change to dark brown, 19 sc.

Round 13: Change to light brown, 1 sc in each st.

Round 14: 1 sc in each st.

Round 15: Change to dark brown, 20 sc, change to light brown, 16 sc, change to dark brown, 18 sc.

Round 16: Change to light brown, 1 sc in each st.

Round 17: 1 sc in each st.

Round 18: Change to dark brown, 21 sc, change to light brown, 15 sc, change to dark brown, 18 sc.

Round 19: Change to light brown, 1 sc in each st.

Round 20: 1 sc in each st.

Round 21: Change to dark brown, 21 sc, change to light brown, 15 sc, change to dark brown, 18 sc.

Round 22: Change to light brown, 1 sc in each st.

Place safety eyes between Rounds 11 and 12, with 9 sts between them. Embroider cheeks using pale pink, and nose using dark brown, following the pictures as a guide **(2)**.

Round 23: [7 sc, sc2tog] to end. (48 sts)

Round 24: 3 sc, sc2tog, [6 sc, sc2tog] 5 times, 3 sc. (42 sts)

Round 25: [5 sc, sc2tog] to end. (36 sts)

Start stuffing the head at this point.

Round 26: 2 sc, sc2tog, [4 sc, sc2tog] 5 times, 2 sc. (30 sts)

Round 27: [3 sc, sc2tog] to end. (24 sts)

Round 28: 1 sc, sc2tog, [2 sc, sc2tog, rep from] 5 times, 1 sc. (18 sts)

Stuff firmly.

Round 29: [1 sc, sc2tog] to end. (12 sts)

Round 30: [Sc2tog] 6 times. (6 sts)

Fasten off and close remaining sts through the front loops (see Techniques: Closing Remaining Stitches Through the Front Loops). Weave in ends (see Techniques: Hiding Ends Inside the Toy).

Ears (make two)

Round 1: Using light brown, 6 sc in a magic ring.

Round 2: 1 sc in each st.

Round 3: 2 sc in each st. (12 sts)

Round 4: 1 sc in each st.

Round 5: [1 sc, 2 sc in next st] rep from * to end. (18 sts)

Round 6: 1 sc in each st.

There is no need to stuff the ears.

Press the opening together with your fingers, with 9 sts on each side and join edges by working 1 sc into each pair of sts (see Techniques: Closing Limbs and Ears).

Fasten off, leaving a long tail for sewing to the head.

Arms (make two)

Round 1: Using light brown, ch 2, 4 sc in the second ch from hook. (4 sts)

Round 2: 2 sc in each st. (8 sts)

Rounds 3–14: 1 sc in each st.

There is no need to stuff the arms.

Press the opening together with your fingers, with 4 sts on each side and join edges by working 1 sc into each pair of sts.

Fasten off, leaving a long tail for sewing to the body.

Tail

Round 1: Using dark brown, 6 sc in a magic ring.

Round 2: 1 sc in each st.

Round 3: 2 sc in each st. (12 sts)

Round 4: 1 sc in each st.

Round 5: [3 sc, 2 sc in next st] to end. (15 sts)

Round 6: 1 sc in each st.

Round 7: Change to light brown, 1 sc in each st.

Round 8: 1 sc in each st.

Round 9: Change to dark brown, 1 sc in each st.

Round 10: 1 sc in each st.

Round 11: [3 sc, sc2tog] to end. (12 sts)

Round 12: Change to light brown, 1 sc in each st.

Round 13: 1 sc in each st.

Start stuffing the tail lightly, just to give it some shape, but not too much or it won't fit the breeches.

Round 14: Change to dark brown, 1 sc in each st.

Round 15: Change to light brown, 1 sc in each st.

Round 16: Change to dark brown, 1 sc in each st.

Round 17: 1 sc in each st.

Round 18: Change to light brown, 1 sc in each st.

Round 19: 1 sc in each st.

Round 20: Change to dark brown, 1 sc in each st.

Rounds 21 and 22: 1 sc in each st.

Round 23: Change to light brown, 1 sc in each st.

Rounds 24 and 25: 1 sc in each st.

Press the opening together with your fingers, with 6 sts on each side and join edges by working 1 sc into each pair of sts.

Fasten off, leaving a long tail for sewing to the back of the body.

Breeches

LEG 1

Round 1: Using light blue, ch 20, 1 sc into the first ch to create a ring, 1 sc into each remaining ch. (20 sts)

Fasten off invisibly and set aside.

LEG 2

Work as for leg 1, but do not fasten off at the end. Continue with the body.

Round 2: Still with leg 2 on your hook, 1 sc, ch 1 and join to leg 1 with a sc **(3)**, pm for new beg of round, 19 sc around leg 1, 1 sc into the 1-ch, 20 sc around leg 2, 1 sc into other side of 1-ch. (42 sts)

Round 3: 3 sc, 2 sc in next st, [6 sc, 2 sc in next st] 5 times, 3 sc. (48 sts)

Rounds 4–7: 1 sc in each st.

Round 8: 3 sc, sc2tog, [6 sc, sc2tog] 5 times, 3 sc. (42 sts)

Round 9: 39 sc. Leave remaining sts unworked.

Round 10: Ch 6, skip 6 sts (the last 3 of Round 9 and first 3 of Round 10), 36 sc (pm in first st), 1 sc in each ch of 6-ch.

Round 11: 8 sc. Leave remaining sts unworked.

Fasten off invisibly and weave in ends.

Jacket

This first part of the jacket will look like a vest and is worked in rows using light blue.

Row 1: Ch 23, 1 sc in the second ch from hook, 1 sc in each ch to end, ch 1, turn. (22 sts)

Row 2: 2 sc, ch 8, skip the next 4 sts (to create first armhole), 10 sc, ch 8, skip the following 4 sts (to create second armhole), 2 sc, ch 1, turn (see Techniques: Creating Armholes on Jackets).

Row 3: 2 sc, 1 sc FLO in each ch of 8-ch, 10 sc, 1 sc FLO in each ch of second 8-ch, 2 sc, ch 1, turn. (30 sts)

Rows 4–8: 1 sc in each st, ch 1, turn.

Row 9: 1 sc in each st.

Row 10: Ch 1, rotate the work 90 degrees clockwise and work 9 sc along the side of the vest, working in the spaces between rows. When you reach the top edge, work 22 sc in the remaining loops of the foundation chain, ch 1, rotate the piece 90 degrees clockwise again and work 9 sc along the other side of the vest, working in the spaces between rows (see Techniques: Edging Flat Pieces).

Fasten off and weave in ends.

Sleeves

The sleeves of the jacket are worked in rounds.

Round 1: Join light blue in one of the remaining loops of the 8-ch from Row 2 of the vest **(4)**, 1 sc in each remaining loop of ch, then 1 sc in each of the 4 sc you skipped before. (12 sts)

Round 2: 1 sc in each st.

Round 3: [2 sc in next st, 5 sc] twice. (14 sts)

Round 4: 1 sc in each st.

Round 5: [2 sc in next st, 6 sc] twice. (16 sts)

Rounds 6–8: 1 sc in each st.

Round 9: 8 sc. Leave remaining sts unworked.

Fasten off and weave in ends.

Repeat these steps for the other sleeve and weave in all ends **(5)**.

Assembly

Embroider the three toes on the feet using dark brown.

Pin the head to the body and sew in place (see Techniques: Attaching Heads). When sewing through the nude part of the neck, work the needle through the back loops of the stitches so the light brown yarn doesn't show.

Embroider vertical stripes on the top of the head using dark brown.

Curve the ears and sew them to the head between Rounds 35 and 34, counted from the closing round.

Sew the arms to the sides of the body between Rounds 26 and 27.

Sew the tail to the back of the body, between rounds 18 and 19.

Slip the breeches onto the legs: you'll need to pull the tail through the hole on the back first, before feeding through the legs.

Slip his arms into the sleeves of the jacket.

Weave in all ends inside the body.

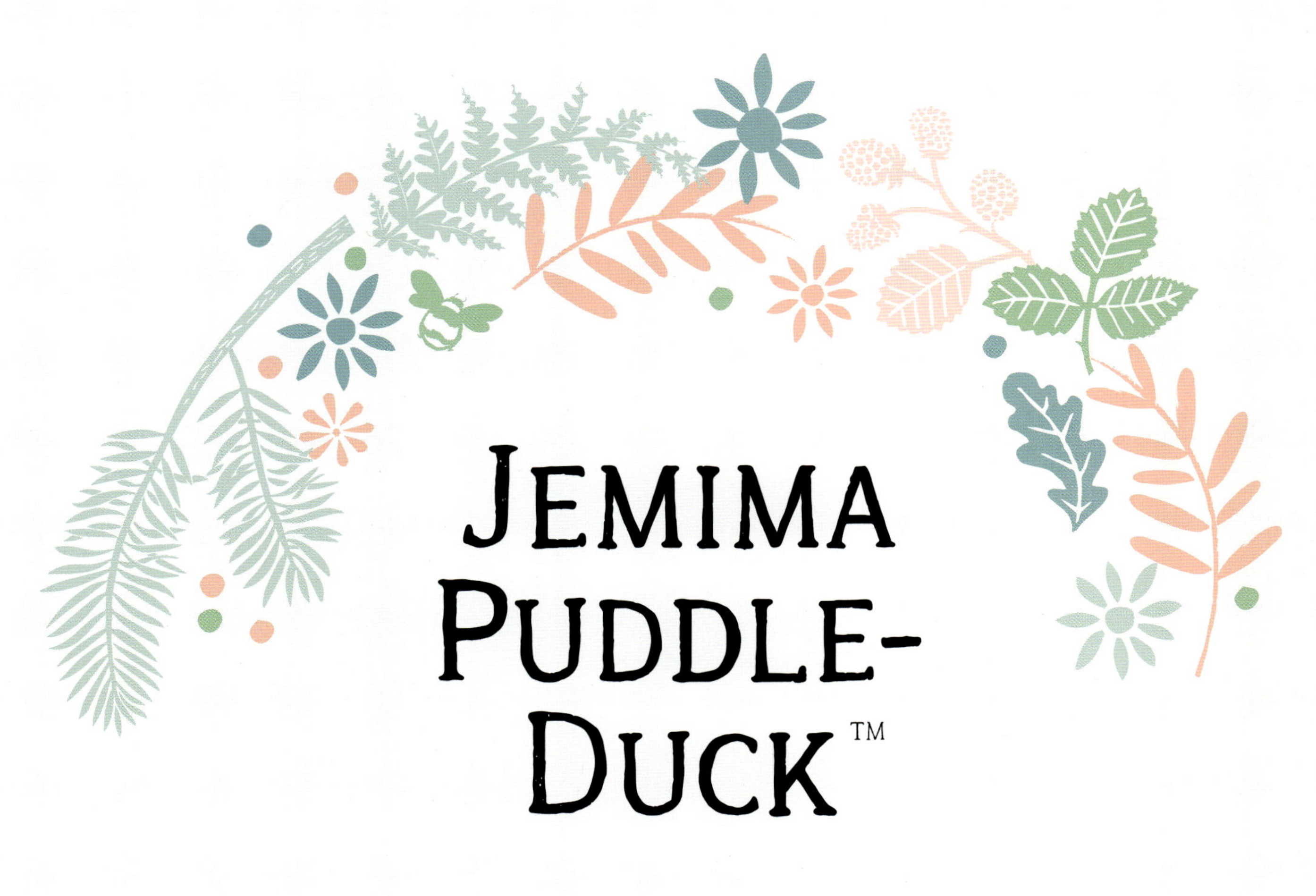

Jemima Puddle-Duck™

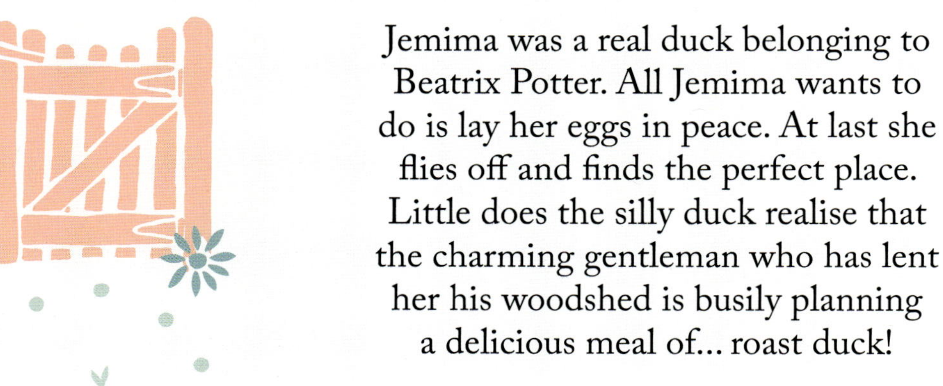

Jemima was a real duck belonging to Beatrix Potter. All Jemima wants to do is lay her eggs in peace. At last she flies off and finds the perfect place. Little does the silly duck realise that the charming gentleman who has lent her his woodshed is busily planning a delicious meal of... roast duck!

Materials

- 3mm (US C/2 or D/3) crochet hook
- 100% 8ply/DK cotton; colours used: yellow; white; light blue; pale pink
- Stitch marker
- 8mm (⅓in) safety eyes
- Yarn needle
- Fibrefill stuffing

Finished size

20cm (7¾in) tall

Beak

Round 1: Using yellow, 6 sc in a magic ring.

Round 2: 1 sc in each st.

Round 3: [1 sc, 2 sc in next st] to end. (9 sts)

Round 4: 1 sc in each st.

Round 5: [2 sc, 2 sc in next st] to end. (12 sts)

Round 6: 1 sc in each st.

Fasten off, leaving a long tail for sewing to the head.

Head and body

Round 1: Using white, 6 sc in a magic ring.

Round 2: 2 sc in each st. (12 sts)

Round 3: [1 sc, 2 sc in next st] to end. (18 sts)

Round 4: 1 sc, 2 sc in next st, [2 sc, 2 sc in next st] 5 times, 1 sc. (24 sts)

Round 5: [3 sc, 2 sc in next st] to end. (30 sts)

Round 6: 2 sc, 2 sc in next st, [4 sc, 2 sc in next st] 5 times, 2 sc. (36 sts)

Round 7: [5 sc, 2 sc in next st] to end. (42 sts)

Rounds 8–20: 1 sc in each st.

Place safety eyes between Rounds 17 and 18 with 8 sts between them **(1)** and opposite the stitch marker. Embroider cheeks using pale pink, following the pictures as a guide.

Round 21: [5 sc, sc2tog] to end. (36 sts)

Start stuffing the head at this point.

Round 22: [1 sc, sc2tog] to end. (24 sts)

Round 23: 1 sc, sc2tog, [2 sc, sc2tog] 5 times, 1 sc. (18 sts)

Round 24: [4 sc, sc2tog] to end. (15 sts)

Rounds 25–29: 1 sc in each st.

Round 30: [4 sc, 2 sc in next st] to end. (18 sts)

Rounds 31–33: 1 sc in each st.

Before working the next round, make sure that your next stitch is in the centre of the back neck **(1)**. If not, work the necessary sts to reach that point.

Round 34: 2 sc in each of the next 3 sts (pm in the first st of this round if you needed to work around to the centre of the back neck, to mark the new beg of round), 12 sc, 2 sc in each of the last 3 sts. (24 sts)

Rounds 35–37: 1 sc in each st.

Stuff the long neck firmly.

Round 38: 2 sc in each of the next 4 sts, 18 sc, 2 sc in each of the last 2 sts. (30 sts)

Rounds 39–41: 1 sc in each st.

Round 42: 2 sc in each of the next 6 sts, 24 sc. (36 sts)

Rounds 43–45: 1 sc in each st.

Round 46: 4 sc, 2 sc in each of the next 6 sts, 26 sc. (42 sts)

Rounds 47–49: 1 sc in each st.

Round 50: 3 sc, 2 sc in next st, [6 sc, 2 sc in next st] 5 times, 3 sc. (48 sts)

Rounds 51–53: 1 sc in each st.

Round 54: 3 sc, sc2tog, [6 sc, sc2tog] 5 times, 3 sc. (42 sts)

Start stuffing the body at this point.

Round 55: [5 sc, sc2tog] to end. (36 sts)

Round 56: [1 sc, sc2tog] to end. (24 sts)

Round 57: 1 sc, sc2tog, [2 sc, sc2tog] 5 times, 1 sc. (18 sts)

Stuff firmly.

Round 58: [1 sc, sc2tog] to end. (12 sts)

Round 59: [Sc2tog] 6 times. (6 sts)

Fasten off and close remaining sts through the front loops (see Techniques: Closing Remaining Stitches Through the Front Loops). Weave in ends (see Techniques: Hiding Ends Inside the Toy).

Wings (make two)

Round 1: Using white, 6 sc in a magic ring.

Round 2: 1 sc in each st.

Round 3: [1 sc, 2 sc in next st] to end. (9 sts)

Rounds 4 and 5: 1 sc in each st.

Round 6: [2 sc, 2 sc in next st] to end. (12 sts)

Rounds 7–11: 1 sc in each st.

There is no need to stuff the wings.

Press the opening together with your fingers, with 6 sts on each side and join edges by working 1 sc into each pair of sts (see Techniques: Closing Limbs and Ears).

Fasten off, leaving a long tail for sewing to the body.

Tail

Round 1: Using white, 6 sc in a magic ring.

Round 2: 1 sc in each st.

Round 3: 2 sc in each st. (12 sts)

Rounds 4 and 5: 1 sc in each st.

Round 6: [1 sc, 2 sc in next st] to end. (18 sts)

Round 7: 1 sc in each st.

There is no need to stuff the tail.

Press the opening together with your fingers, with 9 sts on each side and join edges by working 1 sc into each pair of sts.

Fasten off, leaving a long tail for sewing to the body.

Feet (make two)

Round 1: Using yellow, 6 sc in a magic ring.

Round 2: 1 sc in each st.

Round 3: [1 sc, 2 sc in next st] to end. (9 sts)

Round 4: [2 sc, 2 sc in next st] to end. (12 sts)

Round 5: 1 sc in each st.

Press the opening together with your fingers, with 6 sts on each side and join edges by working 1 sc into each pair of sts.

Fasten off, leaving a long tail for sewing to the body. Using your yarn needle, insert the yarn tails into the feet and exit through the middle of the initial magic ring. Now they are ready for sewing **(2)**.

Poke bonnet

Round 1: Using light blue, 6 sc in a magic ring.

Round 2: 2 sc in each st. (12 sts)

Round 3: 2 sc in each st. (24 sts)

Round 4: [3 sc, 2 sc in next st] to end. (30 sts)

Round 5: 1 sc in each st.

Round 6: 1 sc BLO in each st.

Round 7: 2 sc, 2 sc in next st, [4 sc, 2 sc in next st] 5 times, 2 sc. (36 sts)

Rounds 8–10: 1 sc in each st.

Round 11: [5 sc, 2 sc in next st] to end. (42 sts)

Rounds 12–14: 1 sc in each st.

Round 15: 3 sc, 2 sc in next st, [6 sc, 2 sc in next st] 5 times, 3 sc. (48 sts)

Round 16: 1 sc in each st.

Round 17: [11 sc, 2 sc in next st] to end. (52 sts)

Rounds 18–20: 1 sc in each st.

Round 21: 38 sc BLO, 14 sc.

Now crochet the brim of the bonnet.

Round 22: [1 sc, 2 sc in next st] 19 times, leaving remaining sts unworked, ch 1, turn. (57 sts)

Round 23: 1 sc in each of next 57 sts, ch 1, turn.

Round 24: 1 sc in each of next 57 sts, ch 20 to create first strap.

Fasten off.

Join light blue to the other end of the brim with a slst and ch 20 to create the second strap. Fasten off.

Ruffle

With the bonnet's opening facing away from you, join light blue in the first remaining front loop of Round 21 **(3)**.

Row 1: 3 sc in each remaining front loop of Round 21. (38 sts)

Fasten off and weave in ends (see Techniques: Weaving in Ends) **(4)**.

Tip

The decreases in the shawl are traditional ones, not the invisible ones.

Shawl

The shawl is worked in rows using pale pink.

Row 1: Ch 41, 1 sc in the second ch from hook, 1 sc in each ch to end, ch 1, turn. (40 sts)

Row 2: Sc2tog, 36 sc, sc2tog, ch 1, turn. (38 sts)

Row 3: Sc2tog, 34 sc, sc2tog, ch 1, turn. (36 sts)

Row 4: Sc2tog, 32 sc, sc2tog, ch 1, turn. (34 sts)

Row 5: Sc2tog, 30 sc, sc2tog, ch 1, turn. (32 sts)

Row 6: Sc2tog, 28 sc, sc2tog, ch 1, turn. (30 sts)

Row 7: Sc2tog, 26 sc, sc2tog, ch 1, turn. (28 sts)

Row 8: Sc2tog, 24 sc, sc2tog, ch 1, turn. (26 sts)

Row 9: Sc2tog, 22 sc, sc2tog, ch 1, turn. (24 sts)

Row 10: Sc2tog, 20 sc, sc2tog, ch 1, turn. (22 sts)

Row 11: Sc2tog, 18 sc, sc2tog, ch 1, turn. (20 sts)

Row 12: Sc2tog, 16 sc, sc2tog, ch 1, turn. (18 sts)

Row 13: Sc2tog, 14 sc, sc2tog, ch 1, turn. (16 sts)

Row 14: Sc2tog, 12 sc, sc2tog, ch 1, turn. (14 sts)

Row 15: Sc2tog, 10 sc, sc2tog, ch 1, turn. (12 sts)

Row 16: Sc2tog, 8 sc, sc2tog, ch 1, turn. (10 sts)

Row 17: Sc2tog, 6 sc, sc2tog, ch 1, turn. (8 sts)

Row 18: Sc2tog, 4 sc, sc2tog, ch 1, turn. (6 sts)

Row 19: Sc2tog, 2 sc, sc2tog, ch 1, turn. (4 sts)

Row 20: [Sc2tog] twice, ch 1, turn. (2 sts)

Row 21: Sc2tog, ch 1, turn, rotate the work 90 degrees clockwise and work 21 sc along the side of the triangle, working into the spaces between rows. When you reach the top edge, work 40 sc in the remaining loops of the foundation chain, then ch 1, rotate the piece 90 degrees clockwise again and work 21 sc along the other side of the triangle, working into the spaces between rows (see Techniques: Edging Flat Pieces).

Fasten off and weave in ends **(5)**.

Assembly

Stuff the beak slightly and sew it between the eyes, starting on Round 9 of the head.

Sew the wings to the sides of the body, slightly slanted, starting between Rounds 38 and 39 of the body.

Sew the feet to the base of the body between Rounds 55 and 56.

Using light blue in your yarn needle, embroider tiny flowers to the shawl, following the pictures as a guide, then wrap it around the body. Sew the tips together over her chest or, if you want to make the shawl removable, use a button or a little piece of Velcro.

Place the bonnet on her head and tie the straps together in a bow.

Weave in all ends inside the body.

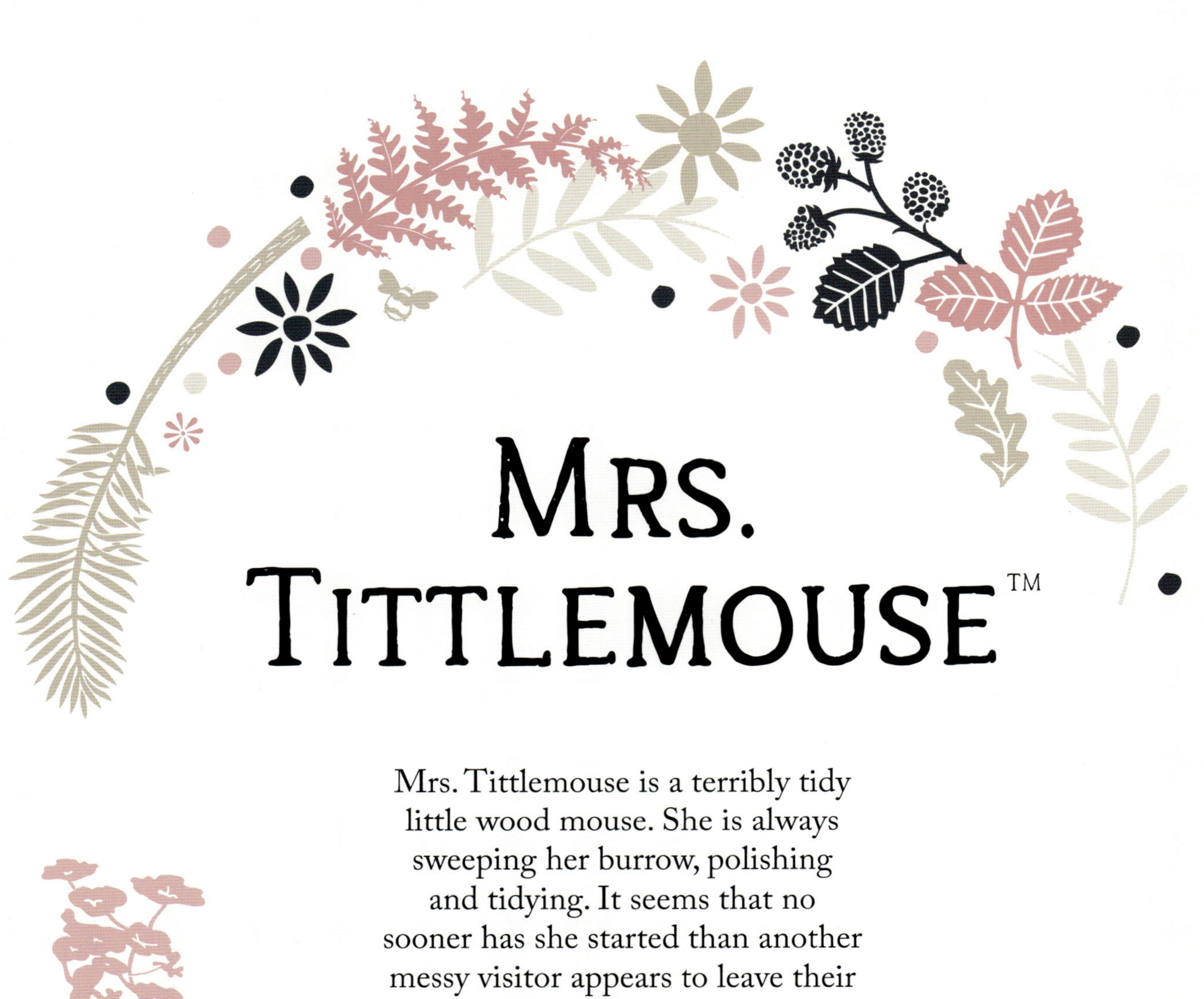

MRS. TITTLEMOUSE™

Mrs. Tittlemouse is a terribly tidy little wood mouse. She is always sweeping her burrow, polishing and tidying. It seems that no sooner has she started than another messy visitor appears to leave their muddy footprints everywhere. Beatrix made beautiful studies of insects, to produce delightful pictures of the spiders to bees found in Mrs. Tittlemouse's home.

Materials

- Size 2.5mm (US B/1 or C/2) crochet hook
- 100% 4ply/fingering cotton; colours used: beige; baby blue; pale pink; toffee; white; dark pink
- Stitch marker
- 6mm (¼in) safety eyes
- Yarn needle
- Fibrefill stuffing

Finished size

9cm (3½in) tall

Base of body

Round 1: Using beige, 6 sc in a magic ring.

Round 2: 2 sc in each st. (12 sts)

Round 3: 2 sc in each st. (24 sts)

Round 4: [3 sc, 2 sc in next st] to end. (30 sts)

Round 5: 1 sc in each st.

Fasten off invisibly (see Techniques: Fastening off Invisibly) and weave in ends (see Techniques: Weaving in Ends). Set aside.

Petticoat and body

Round 1: Using baby blue for the petticoat, ch 30, 1 sc in the last ch from hook to form a ring, making sure not to twist the chain, 1 sc in each ch to end. (30 sts)

Rounds 2 and 3: 1 sc in each st.

Now take the base and place it over the ring, like a lid (wrong side up).

Round 4: 1 sc in each st, working through each st of the petticoat and the base at the same time **(1)**. (30 sts)

Rounds 5–10: 1 sc in each st.

Round 11: Change to pale pink for the dress, 1 sc in each st.

Round 12: 1 sc BLO in each st.

Start stuffing the body at this point.

Round 13: 1 sc in each st.

Round 14: [3 sc, sc2tog] to end. (24 sts)

Round 15: 1 sc in each st.

Round 16: 1 sc, sc2tog, [2 sc, sc2tog] 5 times, 1 sc. (18 sts)

Fasten off, leaving a long tail for sewing to the head.

Skirt

Turn the body upside down and join pale pink in the first remaining front loop of Round 12, at the back of the body.

Round 1: 1 sc FLO in each st of Round 12. (30 sts)

Round 2: [2 sc, 2 sc in next st] to end. (40 sts)

Rounds 3–11: 1 sc in each st.

Fasten off invisibly and weave in ends.

HEAD

Round 1: Using beige, 6 sc in a magic ring.

Round 2: 2 sc in each st. (12 sts)

Round 3: 1 sc in each st.

Round 4: [1 sc, 2 sc in next st] to end. (18 sts)

Round 5: 1 sc in each st.

Round 6: 1 sc, 2 sc in next st, [2 sc, 2 sc in next st] 5 times, 1 sc. (24 sts)

Round 7: 1 sc in each st.

Round 8: [3 sc, 2 sc in next st] to end. (30 sts)

On the next few rounds we will change colour several times. Remember to join the new colour in the last step of the previous st.

Round 9: 14 sc, change to toffee, 2 sc, change to beige, 14 sc.

Round 10: 2 sc, 2 sc in next st, [4 sc, 2 sc in next st] twice, change to toffee, 4 sc, change to beige, 2 sc in next st, [4 sc, 2 sc in next st] twice, 2 sc. (36 sts)

Round 11: [5 sc, 2 sc in next st] twice, 3 sc, change to toffee, 2 sc, 2 sc in next st, 3 sc, change to beige, 2 sc, 2 sc in next st, [5 sc, 2 sc in next st] twice. (42 sts)

Round 12: 16 sc, change to toffee, 9 sc, change to beige, 17 sc.

Round 13: 15 sc, change to toffee, 11 sc, change to beige, 16 sc.

Round 14: 14 sc, change to toffee, 13 sc, change to beige, 15 sc.

Round 15: 13 sc, change to toffee, 15 sc, change to beige, 14 sc.

Place safety eyes between Rounds 7 and 8 with 8 sts between them. Embroider cheeks using pale pink **(2)**.

Round 16: Change to toffee, 1 sc in each st.

Round 17: 1 sc in each st.

Round 18: [5 sc, sc2tog] to end. (36 sts)

Start stuffing the head at this point.

Round 19: 1 sc in each st.

Round 20: 2 sc, sc2tog, [4 sc, sc2tog] 5 times, 2 sc. (30 sts)

Round 21: 1 sc in each st.

Round 22: [3 sc, sc2tog] to end. (24 sts)

Round 23: 1 sc in each st.

Round 24: 1 sc, sc2tog, [2 sc, sc2tog] 5 times, 1 sc. (18 sts)

Stuff firmly.

Round 25: [1 sc, sc2tog] to end. (12 sts)

Round 26: [Sc2tog] 6 times. (6 sts)

Fasten off and close remaining sts through the front loops (see Techniques: Closing Remaining Stitches Through the Front Loops). Weave in ends (see Techniques: Hiding Ends Inside the Toy).

ARMS (make two)

Round 1: Using beige, 6 sc in a magic ring.

Rounds 2–4: 1 sc in each st.

Round 5: Change to pale pink, 1 sc BLO in each st.

There is no need to stuff the arms.

Rounds 6–9: 1 sc in each st.

Press the opening together with your fingers, with 3 sts on each side and join edges by working 1 sc into each pair of sts (see Techniques: Closing Limbs and Ears).

Fasten off, leaving a long tail for sewing to the body.

Ears (make two)

Round 1: Using beige, 6 sc in a magic ring.

Round 2: 2 sc in each st. (12 sts)

Round 3: [1 sc, 2 sc in next st] to end. (18 sts)

Round 4: 1 sc, 2 sc in next st, [2 sc, 2 sc in next st] 5 times, 1 sc. (24 sts)

Fasten off, leaving a long tail for sewing to the head **(3)**.

Tail

Row 1: Using beige, ch 21, 1 sc in the second ch from hook, 1 slst in each ch to end. (20 sts)

Fasten off, leaving a long tail for sewing.

Apron

Row 1: Using white, ch 5, 1 sc in the second ch from hook, 2 sc, 4 sc in the last st (this will allow you to work on the other side of the chain) **(4)**, 3 sc, ch 1, turn. (10 sts)

Row 2: 3 sc, [2 sc in next st] 4 times, 3 sc, ch 1, turn. (14 sts)

Round 3: 5 sc, 2 sc in next st, 3 sc, 2 sc in next st, 4 sc, ch 1, turn. (16 sts)

Round 4: [5 sc, 2 sc in next st] twice, 4 sc. (18 sts)

Fasten off, leaving a long tail for sewing **(5)**.

Collar

Row 1: Using white, ch 21. Starting from the second ch from hook, 3 sc in each st ch to end. (60 sts)

Fasten off, leaving a long tail to knot.

Ribbon

Row 1: Using dark pink, ch 25.

Fasten off.

Assembly

Pin the head to the body and sew in place (see Techniques: Attaching Heads).

Sew the arms to the sides of the body between Rounds 13 and 14.

Sew the ears to the head between Rounds 16 and 17 with 6 stitches between them.

Sew the apron to the waist.

Wrap the collar around the neck and tie it at the back.

Sew the long tail to the beige base of the body.

Make a bow with the ribbon chain and sew it to the back of the dress.

Using a little bit of toffee, embroider some short lines into the ears and some spots around the eyes, following the pictures as a guide.

Weave in all ends inside the body.

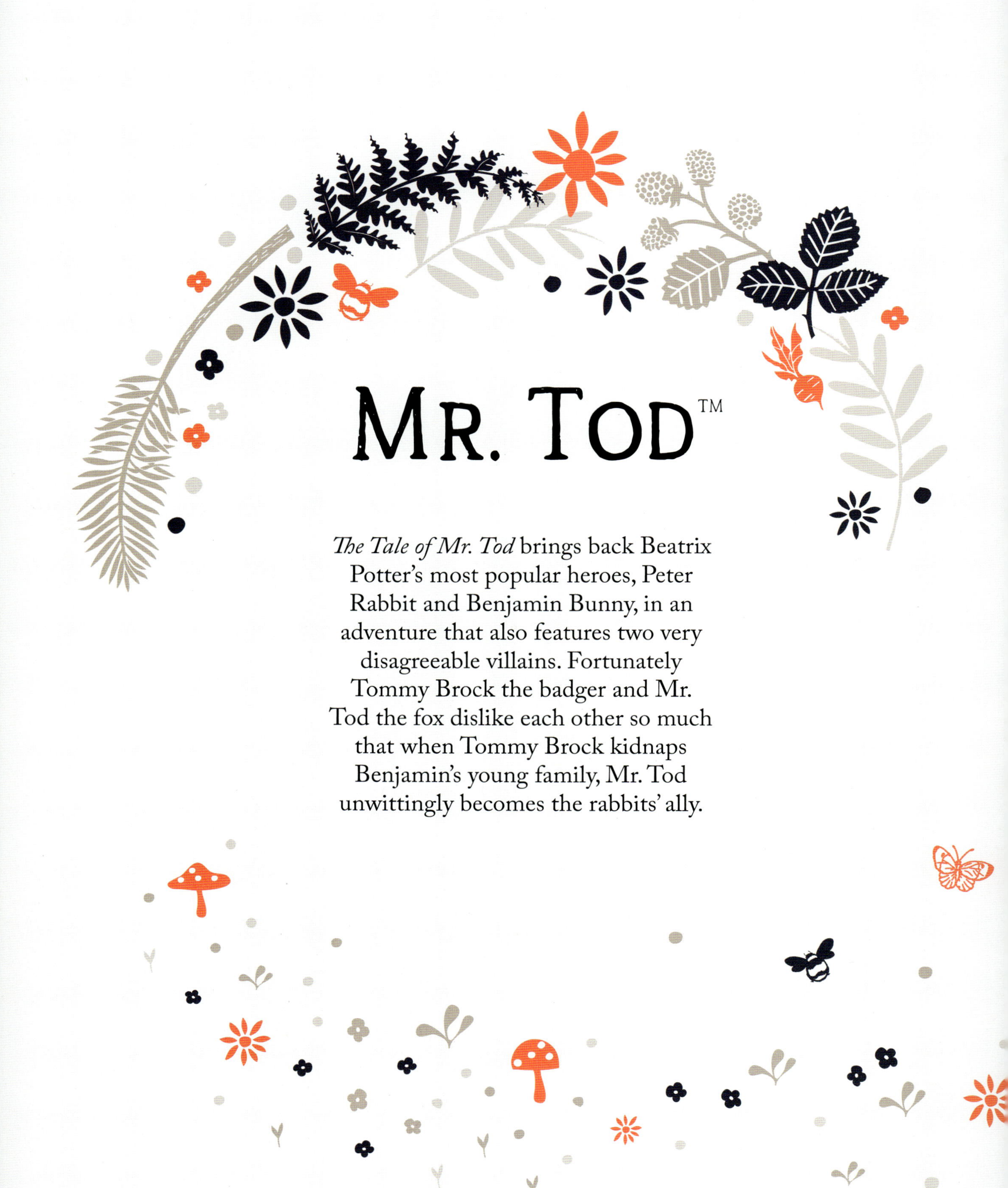

MR. TOD™

The Tale of Mr. Tod brings back Beatrix Potter's most popular heroes, Peter Rabbit and Benjamin Bunny, in an adventure that also features two very disagreeable villains. Fortunately Tommy Brock the badger and Mr. Tod the fox dislike each other so much that when Tommy Brock kidnaps Benjamin's young family, Mr. Tod unwittingly becomes the rabbits' ally.

Materials

- 3mm (US C/2 or D/3) crochet hook
- 100% 8ply/DK cotton; colours used: black; curry yellow; burgundy; beige; burnt orange; white; army green; a small amount of pale pink
- Stitch marker
- 8mm (⅓in) safety eyes
- Yarn needle
- Fibrefill stuffing

Finished size

22cm (8½in) tall

Leg 1

Round 1: Using black, 6 sc in a magic ring. (6 sts)

Round 2: [1 sc, 2 sc in next st] to end. (9 sts)

Round 3: 1 sc BLO in each st.

Rounds 4–9: 1 sc in each st.

Round 10: Change to curry yellow, 1 sc BLO in each st.

Round 11: 2 sc in each st. (18 sts)

Round 12: 1 sc in each st.

Fasten off invisibly (see Techniques: Fastening off Invisibly) and weave in ends (see Techniques: Weaving in Ends). Set aside.

Leg 2

Work as for leg 1, but do not fasten off at the end. Continue with the body.

Body

Round 13: With leg 2 still on your hook, join to leg 1 with a sc **(1)** (see Techniques: Joining Legs), pm for new beg of round, 17 sc around leg 1, 18 sc around leg 2. (36 sts)

Round 14: [5 sc, 2 sc in next st] to end. (42 sts)

Rounds 15–18: 1 sc in each st.

Round 19: [5 sc, sc2tog] to end. (36 sts)

Rounds 20 and 21: 1 sc in each st.

Round 22: Change to burgundy, 1 sc BLO in each st.

Round 23: 2 sc, sc2tog, [4 sc, sc2tog] 5 times, 2 sc. (30 sts)

Rounds 24 and 25: 1 sc in each st.

Round 26: [3 sc, sc2tog] to end. (24 sts)

Rounds 27–29: 1 sc in each st.

Round 30: 1 sc, sc2tog, [2 sc, sc2tog] 5 times, 1 sc. (18 sts)

Start stuffing the body at this point.

Round 31: 1 sc in each st.

On the next few rounds we will change colour several times. Remember to join the new colour in the last step of the previous st.

Round 32: 10 sc, change to beige, 1 sc, change to burgundy, 7 sc.

Round 33: 9 sc, change to beige, 3 sc, change to burgundy, 6 sc.

Round 34: 8 sc, change to beige, 5 sc, change to burgundy, 5 sc.

Round 35: 7 sc, change to beige, 7 sc, change to burgundy, 4 sc.

You should now have a beige triangle at the centre front of Mr. Tod's body.

Fasten off, leaving a long tail for sewing to the head.

Thread a bit of burgundy into your yarn needle and sew two straight stitches at the neck of the vest to mark the edge of the V-neck.

Head

Round 1: Using burnt orange, 6 sc in a magic ring.

Round 2: 2 sc in each st. (12 sts)

On the next few rounds we will change colour several times. Remember to join the new colour in the last step of the previous st.

Round 3: 2 sc in each of the next 4 sts, change to white, 2 sc in each of the next 4 sts, change to burnt orange, 2 sc in each of the last 4 sts. (24 sts)

Round 4: [1 sc, 2 sc in next st] 4 times, change to white, [1 sc, 2 sc in next st] 4 times, change to burnt orange, [1 sc, 2 sc in next st] 4 times. (36 sts)

Round 5: [5 sc, 2 sc in next st] twice, change to white, [5 sc, 2 sc in next st] twice, change to burnt orange, [5 sc, 2 sc in next st] twice. (42 sts)

Round 6: 3 sc, 2 sc in next st, 6 sc, 2 sc in next st, 3 sc, change to white, 3 sc, 2 sc in next st, 6 sc, 2 sc in next st, 3 sc, change to burnt orange, 3 sc, 2 sc in next st, 6 sc, 2 sc in next st, 3 sc. (48 sts)

Rounds 7 and 8: 16 sc, change to white, 16 sc, change to burnt orange, 16 sc.

Round 9: 18 sc, change to white, 12 sc, change to burnt orange, 18 sc.

Round 10: 19 sc, change to white, 10 sc, change to burnt orange, 19 sc.

Rounds 11–22: 1 sc in each st.

Place safety eyes between Rounds 11 and 12 with 9 sts between them. Embroider cheeks using pale pink following the pictures as a guide **(2)**.

Round 23: 3 sc, sc2tog, [6 sc, sc2tog] 5 times, 3 sc. (42 sts)

Round 24: [5 sc, sc2tog] to end. (36 sts)

Start stuffing the head at this point.

Round 25: 2 sc, sc2tog, [4 sc, sc2tog] 5 times, 2 sc. (30 sts)

Round 26: [3 sc, sc2tog] to end. (24 sts)

Round 27: 1 sc, sc2tog, [2 sc, sc2tog] 5 times, 1 sc. (18 sts)

Stuff firmly.

Round 28: [1 sc, sc2tog] to end. (12 sts)

Round 29: [Sc2tog] 6 times. (6 sts)

Fasten off and close remaining sts through the front loops (see Techniques: Closing Remaining Stitches Through the Front Loops). Weave in ends (see Techniques Hiding Ends Inside the Toy).

Nose

Round 1: Using white, 6 sc in a magic ring.

On the next few rounds we will change colour several times. Remember to join the new colour in the last step of the previous st.

Round 2: 2 sc in each of the first 3 sts, change to burnt orange, 2 sc in each of the last 3 sts. (12 sts)

Rounds 3–5: Change to white, 6 sc, change to burnt orange, 6 sc.

Round 6: Change to white, [1 sc, 2 sc in next st] 3 times, change to burnt orange, [1 sc, 2 sc in next st] 3 times. (18 sts)

Round 7: Change to white, 9 sc, change to burnt orange, 9 sc.

Fasten off leaving a long tail for sewing to the head.

1

2

Ears (make two)

Round 1: Using black, 6 sc in a magic ring.

Round 2: 1 sc in each st.

Round 3: Change to burnt orange, 2 sc in each st. (12 sts)

Round 4: 1 sc in each st.

Round 5: [1 sc, 2 sc in next st] twice, change to white, 1 sc, 2 sc in next st, change to burnt orange, [1 sc, 2 sc in next st] 3 times. (18 sts)

Rounds 6 and 7: 6 sc, change to white, 3 sc, change to burnt orange, 9 sc.

Round 8: [1 sc, sc2tog] twice, change to white, 1 sc, sc2tog, change to burnt orange, [1 sc, sc2tog] 3 times. (12 sts)

Round 9: 4 sc, change to white, 2 sc, change to burnt orange, 6 sc.

Round 10: 3 sc. Leave remaining sts unworked.

There is no need to stuff the ears.

Press the opening together with your fingers, with 6 sts on each side and join edges by working 1 sc into each pair of sts (see Techniques: Closing Limbs and Ears).

Fasten off, leaving a long tail for sewing to the head **(3)**.

Tail

Round 1: Using white, 6 sc in a magic ring.

Round 2: 2 sc in each st. (12 sts)

Rounds 3 and 4: 1 sc in each st.

Round 5: [1 sc, 2 sc in next st] to end. (18 sts)

Rounds 6 and 7: 1 sc in each st.

Round 8: Change to burnt orange, 1 sc in each st.

Rounds 9–11: 1 sc in each st.

Round 12: 2 sc, sc2tog, [4 sc, sc2tog] twice, 2 sc. (15 sts)

Stuff firmly.

Rounds 13 and 14: 1 sc in each st.

Round 15: [3 sc, sc2tog] to end. (12 sts)

Rounds 16–23: 1 sc in each st.

Round 24: 4 sc. Leave remaining sts unworked.

Press the opening together with your fingers, with 6 sts on each side and join edges by working 1 sc into each pair of sts.

Fasten off, leaving a long tail for sewing to the back of the body **(4)**.

Arms (make two)

Round 1: Using burnt orange, ch 2, 4 sc in the second ch from hook. (4 sts)

Round 2: 2 sc in each st. (8 sts)

Rounds 3–5: 1 sc in each st.

Round 6: Change to army green, 1 sc BLO in each st.

There is no need to stuff the arms.

Rounds 7–16: 1 sc in each st.

Press the opening together with your fingers, with 4 sts on each side and join edges by working 1 sc into each pair of sts.

Fasten off, leaving a long tail for sewing to the body.

Coat

The coat is actually a long vest, but when you put it on Mr. Tod it will look like a coat because of his burnt orange and army green arms. The vest is worked in rows from the top down, using army green.

Row 1: Ch 21, 1 sc in the second ch from hook, 1 sc in each ch to end, ch 1, turn. (20 sts)

Row 2: 1 sc in each st, ch 1, turn.

Row 3: 3 sc, ch 6, skip the following 4 sts (to create first armhole), 6 sc, ch 6, skip the following 4 sts (to create second armhole), 3 sc, ch 1, turn (see Techniques: Creating Armholes on Jackets).

Row 4: 3 sc, 1 sc in each ch of 6-ch, 6 sc, 1 sc in each ch of second 6-ch, 3 sc, ch 1, turn. (24 sts)

Rows 5 and 6: 1 sc in each st, ch 1, turn.

Row 7: 2 sc in next st, 5 sc, 2 sc in next st, 10 sc, 2 sc in next st, 5 sc, 2 sc in next st, ch 1, turn. (28 sts)

Rows 8 and 9: 1 sc in each st, ch 1, turn.

Row 10: 2 sc in next st, 6 sc, 2 sc in next st, 12 sc, 2 sc in next st, 6 sc, 2 sc in next st, ch 1, turn. (32 sts)

Rows 11 and 12: 1 sc in each st, ch 1, turn.

Row 13: 2 sc in next st, 7 sc, 2 sc in next st, 14 sc, 2 sc in next st, 7 sc, 2 sc in next st, ch 1, turn. (36 sts)

Row 14: 1 sc in each st, ch 1, turn.

Row 15: 1 sc in each st.

Row 16: Ch 1, rotate the work 90 degrees clockwise and work 15 sc along the side of the vest, working into the spaces between rows. When you reach the top edge, work 20 sc in the remaining loops of the foundation chain, then ch 1, rotate the piece 90 degrees clockwise again and work 15 sc along the other side of the vest, working into the spaces between rows (see Techniques: Edging Flat Pieces).

Fasten off and weave in ends.

Ribbon

Row 1: Using beige, ch 25.

Fasten off.

Assembly

Stuff the nose slightly and sew it between the eyes, matching the white areas on both pieces.

Pin the head to the body and sew in place (see Techniques: Attaching Heads). When sewing through the beige part of the neck, work the needle through the back loops of the stitches, so the burgundy yarn doesn't show.

Sew the arms to the sides of the body between Rounds 33 and 34.

Count 8 rounds down from the last round of the head, and sew the ears here, between this round and the one below.

Sew the tail to the back of the body, right where the burgundy vest begins.

Make a bow with the ribbon chain and sew it to the neck **(5)**.

Slip his arms into the armholes of the coat.

Weave in all ends inside the body.

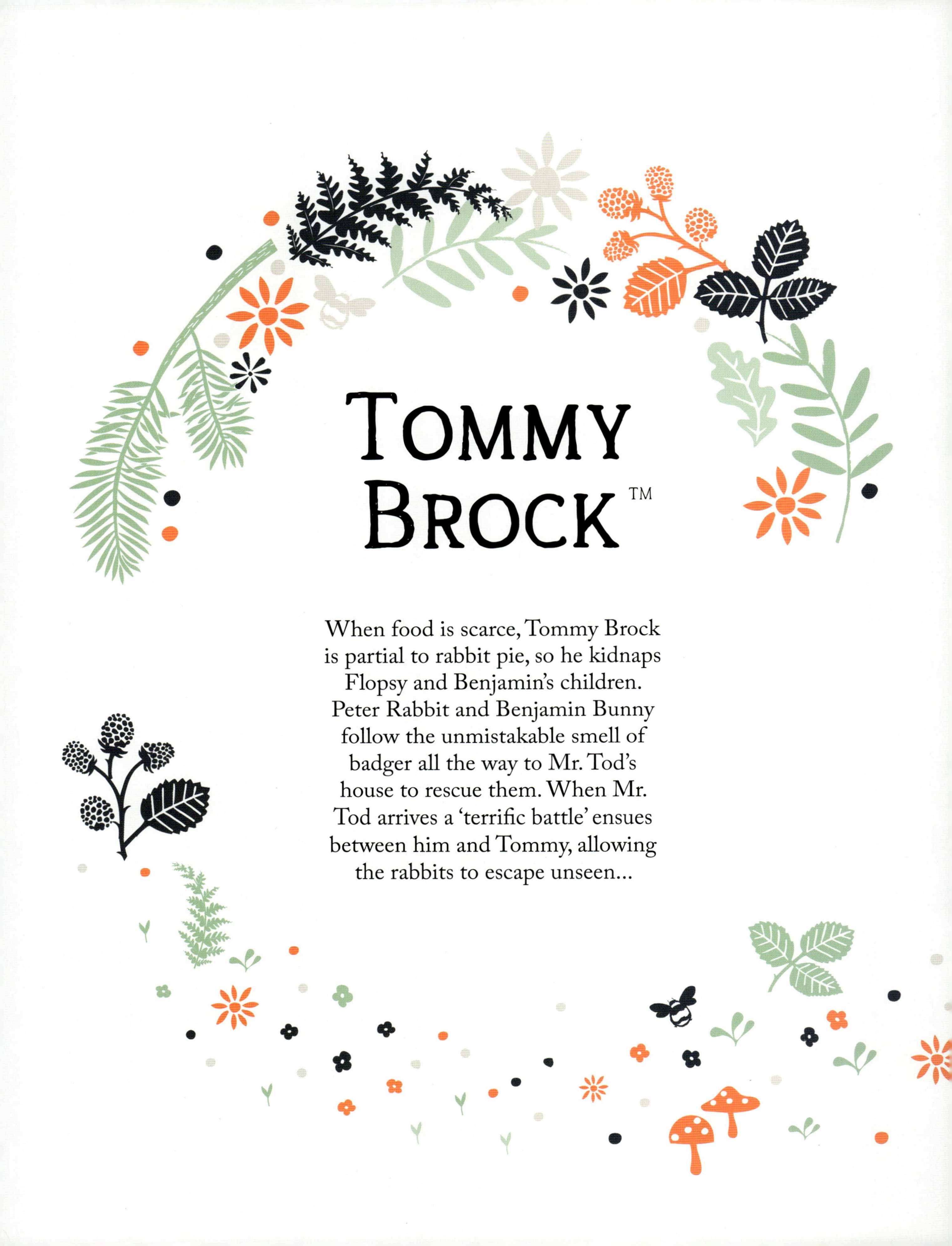

Tommy Brock™

When food is scarce, Tommy Brock is partial to rabbit pie, so he kidnaps Flopsy and Benjamin's children. Peter Rabbit and Benjamin Bunny follow the unmistakable smell of badger all the way to Mr. Tod's house to rescue them. When Mr. Tod arrives a 'terrific battle' ensues between him and Tommy, allowing the rabbits to escape unseen...

Materials

- 3mm (US C/2 or D/3) crochet hook
- 100% 8ply/DK cotton; colours used: dark brown; mustard; dark rose; white; black; denim blue; sage green; a small amount of pale pink
- Stitch marker
- 8mm (⅓in) safety eyes
- Yarn needle
- Fibrefill stuffing

Finished size

15cm (6in) tall

Leg 1

Round 1: Using dark brown for the boots, ch 6, 2 sc in the second ch from hook, 3 sc, 4 sc in next st (this will allow you to work on the other side of the chain), 3 sc, 2 sc in the last st. (14 sts)

Round 2: [1 sc, 2 sc in next st, 4 sc, 2 sc in next st] twice. (18 sts)

Round 3: 1 sc BLO in each st.

Round 4: 7 sc, [sc2tog] twice, 7 sc. (16 sts)

Round 5: 6 sc, sc2tog, 1 sc, sc2tog, 5 sc. (14 sts)

Round 6: 4 sc, sc2tog, 2 sc, sc2tog, 4 sc. (12 sts)

Round 7: 1 sc in each st.

Round 8: Change to mustard, 1 sc BLO in each st.

Round 9: [1 sc, 2 sc in next st] to end. (18 sts)

Round 10: 6 sc. Leave remaining sts unworked.

Fasten off invisibly (see Techniques: Fastening off Invisibly) and weave in ends (see Techniques: Weaving in Ends). Set aside.

Leg 2

Work as for leg 1, but do not fasten off at the end. Continue with the body.

Body

Round 11: With leg 2 still on your hook, join to leg 1 with a sc **(1)** (see Techniques: Joining Legs), pm here for new beg of round (IMPORTANT: make sure both feet point away from you), 17 sc around leg 1, 18 sc around leg 2. (36 sts)

Round 12: [5 sc, 2 sc in next st] to end. (42 sts)

Rounds 13–16: 1 sc in each st.

Round 17: Change to dark rose, 1 sc BLO in each st.

Round 18: 1 sc in each st.

Round 19: [5 sc, sc2tog] to end. (36 sts)

Rounds 20 and 21: 1 sc in each st.

Round 22: 2 sc, sc2tog, [4 sc, sc2tog] 5 times, 2 sc. (30 sts)

Rounds 23 and 24: 1 sc in each st.

Round 25: [3 sc, sc2tog] to end. (24 sts)

Round 26: 1 sc in each st.

Start stuffing the body at this point.

Round 27: 1 sc, sc2tog, [2 sc, sc2tog] 5 times, 1 sc. (18 sts)

Fasten off, leaving a long tail for sewing to the head.

HEAD

Round 1: Using white, 6 sc in a magic ring.

Round 2: 2 sc in each st. (12 sts)

Rounds 3 and 4: 1 sc in each st.

On the next few rounds we will change colour several times. Remember to join the new colour in the last step of the previous st.

Round 5: 3 sc, change to black, 2 sc, change to white, 4 sc, change to black, 2 sc, change to white, 1 sc.

Round 6: 1 sc, 2 sc in next st, 1 sc, change to black, 1 sc, 2 sc in next st, change to white, 2 sc in next st, 1 sc, 2 sc in next st, 1 sc, change to black, 2 sc in next st, 1 sc, change to white, 2 sc in next st. (18 sts)

Round 7: 4 sc, change to black, 3 sc, change to white, 6 sc, change to black, 3 sc, change to white, 2 sc.

Round 8: 2 sc, 2 sc in next st, 1 sc, change to black, 1 sc, 2 sc in next st, 1 sc, change to white, 1 sc, 2 sc in next st, 2 sc, 2 sc in next st, 1 sc, change to black, 1 sc, 2 sc in next st, 1 sc, change to white, 1 sc, 2 sc in next st. (24 sts)

Round 9: 5 sc, change to black, 4 sc, change to white, 8 sc, change to black, 4 sc, change to white, 3 sc.

Round 10: 3 sc, 2 sc in next st, 1 sc, change to black, 2 sc, 2 sc in next st, 1 sc, change to white, 2 sc, 2 sc in next st, 3 sc, 2 sc in next st, 1 sc, change to black, 2 sc, 2 sc in next st, 1 sc, change to white, 2 sc, 2 sc in next st. (30 sts)

Round 11: 6 sc, change to black, 5 sc, change to white, 10 sc, change to black, 5 sc, change to white, 4 sc.

Round 12: 4 sc, 2 sc in next st, 1 sc, change to black, 3 sc, 2 sc in next st, 1 sc, change to white, 3 sc, 2 sc in next st, 4 sc, 2 sc in next st, 1 sc, change to black, 3 sc, 2 sc in next st, 1 sc, change to white, 3 sc, 2 sc in next st. (36 sts)

Round 13: 5 sc, 2 sc in next st, 1 sc, change to black, 4 sc, 2 sc in next st, 1 sc, change to white, 4 sc, 2 sc in next st, 5 sc, 2 sc in next st, 1 sc, change to black, 4 sc, 2 sc in next st, 1 sc, change to white, 4 sc, 2 sc in next st. (42 sts)

Round 14: 6 sc, 2 sc in next st, 1 sc, change to black, 5 sc, 2 sc in next st, 1 sc, change to white, 5 sc, 2 sc in next st, 6 sc, 2 sc in next st, 1 sc, change to black, 5 sc, 2 sc in next st, 1 sc, change to white, 5 sc, 2 sc in next st. (48 sts)

Rounds 15–18 : 9 sc, change to black, 8 sc, change to white, 16 sc, change to black, 8 sc, change to white, 7 sc **(2)**.

Place safety eyes between Rounds 9 and 10, into the black areas, with 12 sts between them. Embroider a white line around half of each eye to enhance them, then embroider cheeks using pale pink.

Round 19: 3 sc, sc2tog, [6 sc, sc2tog] 5 times, 3 sc. (42 sts)

Round 20: [5 sc, sc2tog] to end. (36 sts)

Start stuffing the head at this point.

Round 21: 2 sc, sc2tog, [4 sc, sc2tog] 5 times, 2 sc. (30 sts)

Round 22: [3 sc, sc2tog] to end. (24 sts)

Round 23: 1 sc, sc2tog, [2 sc, sc2tog] 5 times, 1 sc. (18 sts)

Stuff firmly.

Round 24: [1 sc, sc2tog] to end. (12 sts)

Round 25: [Sc2tog] 6 times. (6 sts)

Fasten off and close remaining sts through the front loops (see Techniques: Closing Remaining Stitches Through the Front Loops). Weave in ends (see Techniques: Hiding Ends Inside the Toy).

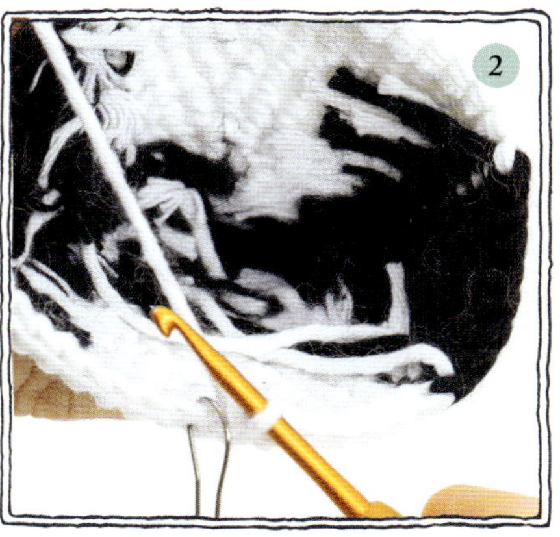

EARS (make two)

Round 1: Using white, ch 2, 4 sc in the second ch from hook. (4 sts)

Round 2: 2 sc in each st. (8 sts)

Round 3: 1 sc in each st.

There is no need to stuff the ears.

Press the opening together with your fingers, with 4 sts on each side and join edges by working 1 sc into each pair of sts (see Techniques: Closing Limbs and Ears).

Fasten off, leaving a long tail for sewing to the head.

ARMS (make two)

Round 1: Using black, ch 2, 4 sc in the second ch from hook. (4 sts)

Round 2: 2 sc in each st. (8 sts)

Rounds 3–5: 1 sc in each st.

Round 6: Change to denim blue, 1 sc BLO in each st.

There is no need to stuff the arms.

Rounds 7–14: 1 sc in each st.

Press the opening together with your fingers, with 4 sts on each side and join edges by working 1 sc into each pair of sts.

Fasten off, leaving a long tail for sewing to the body.

JACKET

The jacket is actually a vest, but when you put it on him it will look like a jacket because of his black and denim blue arms. The vest is worked in rows from the top down, using denim blue.

Row 1: Ch 25, 1 sc in the second ch from hook, 1 sc in each ch to end, ch 1, turn. (24 sts)

Rows 2 and 3: 1 sc in each st, ch 1, turn.

Row 4: 3 sc, ch 6, skip the following 4 sts (to create first armhole), 10 sc, ch 6, skip the following 4 sts (to create second armhole), 3 sc, ch 1, turn (see Techniques: Creating Armholes on Jackets).

Row 5: 3 sc, 1 sc in each ch of 6-ch, 10 sc, 1 sc in each ch of second 6-ch, 3 sc, ch 1, turn. (28 sts)

Rows 6 and 7: 1 sc in each st, ch 1, turn.

Row 8: 2 sc in next st, 6 sc, 2 sc in next st, 12 sc, 2 sc in next st, 6 sc, 2 sc in next st, ch 1, turn. (32 sts)

Rows 9 and 10: 1 sc in each st, ch 1, turn.

Row 11: 2 sc in next st, 7 sc, 2 sc in next st, 14 sc, 2 sc in next st, 7 sc, 2 sc in next st, ch 1, turn. (36 sts)

Rows 12 and 13: 1 sc in each st, ch 1, turn.

Row 14: 1 sc in each st.

Row 15: Ch 1, rotate the work 90 degrees clockwise and work 13 sc along the side of the vest, working into the spaces between rows. When you reach the top edge, work 20 sc in the remaining loops of the foundation chain, then ch 1, rotate the piece 90 degrees clockwise again and work 13 sc along the other side of the vest, working into the spaces between rows (see Techniques: Edging Flat Pieces).

Fasten off and weave in ends **(3)**.

Scarf

Row 1: Using sage green, ch 47, 1 sc in the second ch from hook, 1 sc in each ch to end, ch 1, turn. (46 sts)

Row 2: 1 sc BLO in each st.

Fasten off and weave in ends **(4)**.

Assembly

Embroider the nose to the tip of the head using black, following the pictures as a guide.

Pin the head to the body and sew in place (see Techniques: Attaching Heads).

Sew the arms to the sides of the body between Rounds 25 and 26.

Curve the ears a bit and sew them to the head between Rounds 18 and 19, with 13 stitches between them.

Tie the scarf around the neck.

Slip his arms through the armholes of the jacket.

Using black, embroider laces on the boots.

Weave in all ends inside the body.

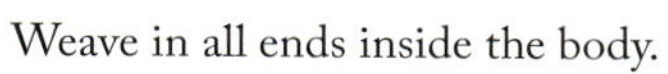

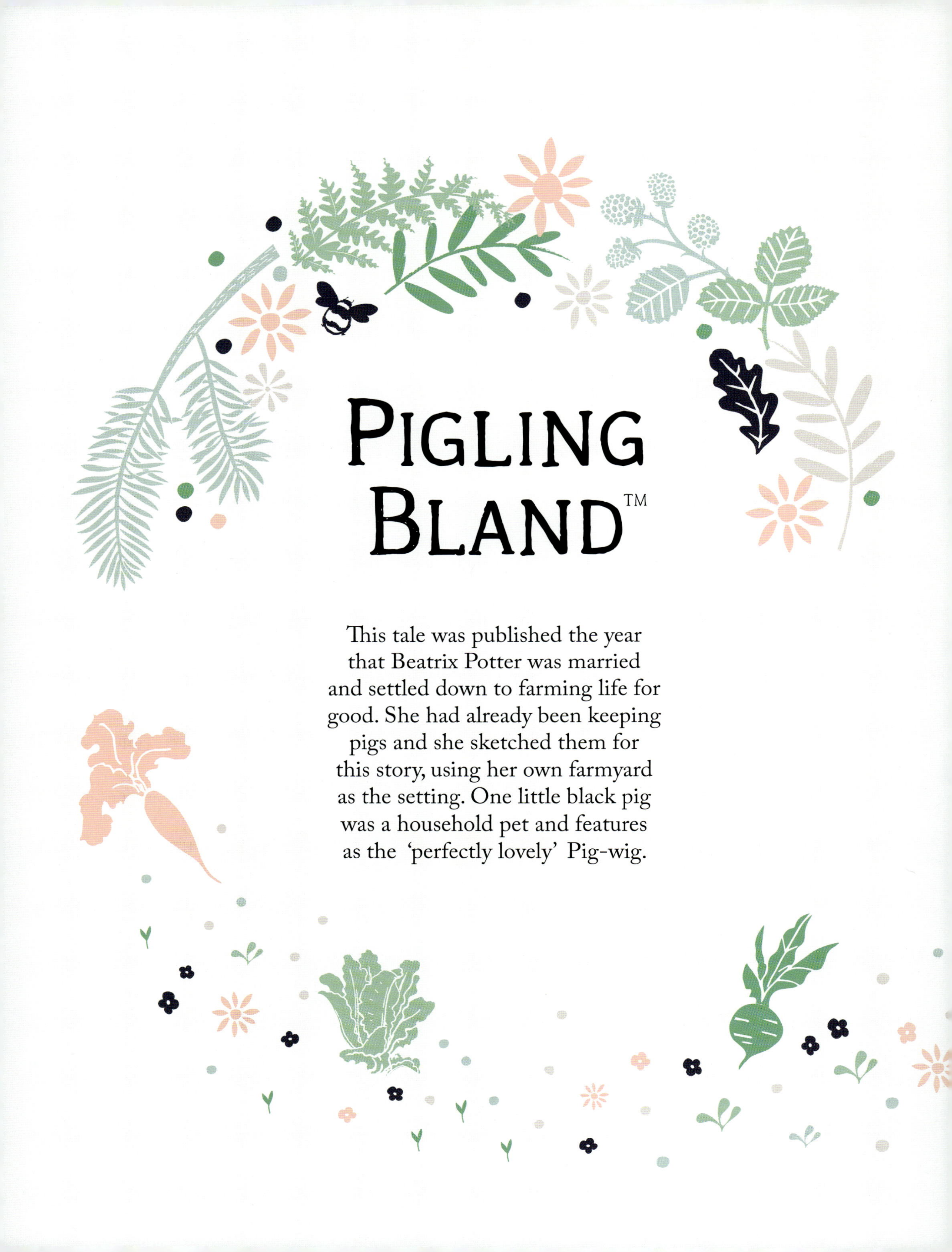

Pigling Bland™

This tale was published the year that Beatrix Potter was married and settled down to farming life for good. She had already been keeping pigs and she sketched them for this story, using her own farmyard as the setting. One little black pig was a household pet and features as the 'perfectly lovely' Pig-wig.

Materials

- 3mm (US C/2 or D/3) crochet hook
- 100% 8ply/DK cotton; colours used: curry yellow; light blue; white; pale pink; dark rose; a small amount of pink and dark brown
- Stitch marker
- Yarn needle
- 8mm (⅓in) safety eyes
- Fibrefill stuffing

Finished size

22cm (8½in) tall

Body

Round 1: Using curry yellow for the shorts, 6 sc in a magic ring.

Round 2: 2 sc in each st. (12 sts)

Round 3: 2 sc in each st. (24 sts)

Round 4: *1 sc, 2 sc in next st; rep from * to end. (36 sts)

Round 5: *5 sc, 2 sc in next st; rep from * to end. (42 sts)

Round 6: 3 sc, 2 sc in next st, [6 sc, 2 sc in next st] 5 times, 3 sc. (48 sts)

Rounds 7–13: 1 sc in each st.

Round 14: 3 sc, sc2tog, [6 sc, sc2tog] 5 times, 3 sc. (42 sts)

Rounds 15–17: 1 sc in each st.

Round 18: Change to light blue for the vest, 1 sc BLO in each st.

Round 19: 1 sc in each st.

Round 20: *5 sc, sc2tog; rep from * to end. (36 sts)

Rounds 21–23: 1 sc in each st.

Round 24: 2 sc, sc2tog, [4 sc, sc2tog] 5 times, 2 sc. (30 sts)

Rounds 25–27: 1 sc in each st.

Round 28: *3 sc, sc2tog; rep from * to end. (24 sts)

Start stuffing the body at this point.

Round 29: 1 sc, sc2tog, [2 sc, sc2tog] 5 times, 1 sc. (18 sts)

Round 30: Change to white, 1 sc in each st.

Round 31: Change to pale pink, 1 sc BLO in each st.

Round 32: 1 sc BLO in each st.

Rounds 33–35: 1 sc in each st.

Round 36: *1 sc, sc2tog; rep from * to end. (12 sts)

Stuff the neck firmly.

Round 37: [Sc2tog] 6 times. (6 sts)

Fasten off and close remaining sts through the front loops (see Techniques: Closing Remaining Stitches Through the Front Loops). Weave in ends (see Techniques: Weaving in Ends).

Collar

With the neck end facing down, join white in the first remaining front loop of Round 31 at the back of the neck.

Round 1: 1 sc FLO in each st of Round 31. (18 sts)

Round 2: 6 sc, (1 hdc, 1 dc) in next st, 3 dc in next st, 1 slst **(1)**, (1 slst, ch 2, 2 dc) in next st, (1 dc, 1 hdc) in next st, 7 sc. (24 sts, excluding ch)

Fasten off invisibly (see Techniques: Fastening off Invisibly) and weave in ends (see Techniques: Hiding Ends Inside the Toy).

HEAD

With the neck end of the body up, join pale pink in the first remaining front loop of Round 32 at the back of the neck.

Round 1: 2 sc FLO in each st of Round 32. (36 sts)

Round 2: [3 sc, 2 sc in next st] to end. (45 sts)

Round 3: [4 sc, 2 sc in next st] to end. (54 sts)

Rounds 4–19: 1 sc in each st.

Place safety eyes between Rounds 7 and 8 with 8 sts between them. Embroider cheeks using pink.

Round 20: *7 sc, sc2tog; rep from * to end. (48 sts)

Round 21: 3 sc, sc2tog, [6 sc, sc2tog] 5 times, 3 sc. (42 sts)

Round 22: *5 sc, sc2tog; rep from * to end. (36 sts)

Start stuffing the head at this point.

Round 23: 2 sc, sc2tog, [4 sc, sc2tog] 5 times, 2 sc. (30 sts)

Round 24: *3 sc, sc2tog; rep from * to end. (24 sts)

Round 25: 1 sc, sc2tog, [2 sc, sc2tog] 5 times, 1 sc. (18 sts)

Stuff firmly.

Round 26: *1 sc, sc2tog; rep from * to end. (12 sts)

Round 27: [Sc2tog] 6 times. (6 sts)

Fasten off and close remaining sts through the front loops. Weave in ends.

NOSE

Round 1: Using pale pink, 5 sc in a magic ring.

Round 2: 2 sc in each st. (10 sts)

Round 3: [1 sc, 2 sc in next st] to end. (15 sts)

Round 4: 1 sc BLO in each st.

Round 5: 1 sc in each st.

Fasten off leaving a long tail for sewing to the head.

EARS (make two)

Round 1: Using pale pink, 6 sc in a magic ring.

Round 2: 1 sc in each st.

Round 3: 2 sc in each st. (12 sts)

Rounds 4 and 5: 1 sc in each st.

Round 6: *1 sc, 2 sc in next st; rep from * to end. (18 sts)

Round 7: 1 sc in each st.

There is no need to stuff the ears.

Press the opening together with your fingers, with 9 sts on each side and join edges by working 1 sc into each pair of sts (see Techniques: Closing Limbs and Ears).

Fasten off, leaving a long tail for sewing to the head **(2)**.

Arms (make two)

Round 1: Using pale pink, 5 sc in a magic ring.

Round 2: 2 sc in each st. (10 sts)

Rounds 3–6: 1 sc in each st.

Round 7: Change to dark rose, 1 sc BLO in each st.

There is no need to stuff the arms.

Rounds 8–15: 1 sc in each st.

Press the opening together with your fingers, with 5 sts on each side and join edges by working 1 sc into each pair of sts.

Fasten off, leaving a long tail for sewing to the body.

Legs (make two)

Round 1: Using pale pink, 5 sc in a magic ring.

Round 2: 2 sc in each st. (10 sts)

Round 3: 1 sc BLO in each st.

Rounds 4–11: 1 sc in each st.

Round 12: Change to curry yellow, 1 sc BLO in each st.

Stuff the legs firmly. Fasten off, leaving a long tail for sewing to the body.

Jacket

The jacket is actually a vest, but when you put it on him it will look like a jacket because of his pale pink and dark rose arms. The vest is worked in rows from the top down, using dark rose.

Row 1: Ch 25, 1 sc in the second ch from hook, 1 sc in each ch to end, ch 1, turn. (24 sts)

Row 2: 1 sc in each st, ch 1, turn.

Row 3: 3 sc, ch 8, skip the following 4 sts (to create first armhole), 10 sc, ch 8, skip the following 4 sts (to create second armhole), 3 sc, ch 1, turn (see Techniques: Creating Armholes on Jackets).

Row 4: 3 sc, 1 sc in each ch of 8-ch, 10 sc, 1 sc in each ch of second 8-ch, 3 sc, ch 1, turn. (32 sts)

Rows 5–15: 1 sc in each st, ch 1, turn.

Row 16: 1 sc in each st.

Row 17: Ch 1, rotate the work 90 degrees clockwise and work 16 sc along the side of the vest, working into the spaces between rows. When you reach the top edge, work 24 sc in the remaining loops of the foundation chain, then ch 1, rotate the piece 90 degrees clockwise again and work 16 sc along the other side of the vest, working into the spaces between rows (see Techniques: Edging Flat Pieces).

Fasten off and weave in ends **(3)**.

Assembly

Sew the nose between the eyes. Then with a bit of dark brown, embroider the nostrils **(4)**.

Sew the ears to the head, starting on Round 14 and ending on Round 23. The tips of the ears should point forward and lie flat on the head.

Sew the arms to the sides of the body between Rounds 26 and 27.

Sew the legs to the base of the body **(5)**.

Slip his arms through the armholes of the jacket.

Weave in all ends inside the body.

Techniques

Here you will find all of the techniques and tutorials that you need to create Peter Rabbit and his friends, plus their accessories. I have included an explanation for each technique, along with lots of photos, so that you can follow them easily. You may prefer to use your own methods, and that's fine too, but they're here if you need them and I hope they help you with the placement of your hook or stitches and to sew your toys together.

Tip

An invisible single crochet decrease can be used to make your decreasing less visible by crocheting into the front loops only of the stitches being worked.

Anatomy of a Stitch

The top of every finished stitch looks like a sideways letter V, with two loops meeting at one end **(1)**. The loop closer to you is the front loop and the loop behind it is the back loop. You will sometimes be asked to crochet certain stitches in the front loops only (FLO) or in the back loops only (BLO) and there's always a reason for this: sometimes it's to mark the end of a section in a certain colour or to leave a loop to crochet into for a different part of the design.

Increasing

This means working two stitches in the same stitch **(2)**. After you have worked the first stitch, you simply insert your hook back into the same place and work the next stitch.

Invisible Single Crochet Decrease

An invisible decrease means working two stitches together at the same time so that it goes unnoticed. Insert the hook in the front loop of the next stitch **(3)** and in the front loop of the stitch next to that, one at a time **(4)**. Yarn over hook and draw it through both front loops in one go. Yarn over hook again and draw it through the two remaining loops on your hook **(5)**. The invisible single crochet decrease only works for three-dimensional pieces that will be stuffed later.

Regular Single Crochet Decrease

To crochet the shawl used by Jemima Puddle-Duck, which is a flat piece, you should use a regular single crochet decrease, which is worked in the same way as an invisible single crochet decrease, but you insert your hook under both loops of the stitches instead of just the front loops.

Changing colour

To change to another colour you should join the new colour during the final step of the last stitch worked in the old colour. This means that when the last two loops of the stitch remain on your hook, you should grab the new colour, wrap it around your hook **(6)** and pull it through those two loops. This will leave the new colour on your hook **(7)**, ready to work the next stitch in that colour **(8)**.

When working pieces that will be stuffed later, I cut the yarn of the old colour and knot it together with the new colour on the inside, to secure both tails. This can only be done in three-dimensional pieces, of course, because these knots will remain inside the toy and won't be visible **(9)**. When working flat pieces that have a right and wrong side, you will have to weave in the ends in between the stitches on the wrong side.

Some animals in this book, like the rabbits, have several colour changes and you might prefer to carry the yarn inside instead of cutting and knotting. This is known as the 'tapestry technique', and it works better when you don't carry the yarn for long distances.

Fastening off invisibly

This method avoids the little stub that can look unsightly when you fasten off your crochet. When you have your final loop on the hook and have finished your crochet, cut the yarn, take it over the hook and pull all the way through the final loop. Pull the yarn tight, which creates a small knot. Thread the yarn tail onto a yarn needle and insert the needle, from the back of the work, underneath the top V of the second stitch along the main edge **(10)**. Pull the yarn all the way through. Insert the needle from the front, into the top V of the last stitch made, and pull through **(11)**. You have created a 'mimic' stitch that covers the small knot and joins up the round neatly.

Closing remaining stitches through the front loops

After the final round, you may be instructed to close the remaining stitches through the front loops. To do this, fasten off after the last stitch and thread the yarn onto a yarn needle. Insert the needle through each front loop of the last round of stitches (through one loop of the stitch only) **(1)**. When you reach the end, pull gently to close up the gap **(2)**. Secure the thread with a few stitches and hide the ends inside the toy.

Hiding ends inside the toy

Insert your crochet hook into the toy, in between stitches, about 5cm (2in) from the tail end that you want to hide, then push the hook out between stitches that are close to the tail end, making sure that the hook is really close to the tail end of yarn. Take the yarn over the hook **(3)** and pull through the toy – as you pull out your hook, the yarn will come with it. Snip the yarn close to the toy to leave a clean finish **(4)**.

Working in rows

Flat pieces are worked in rows, starting with a foundation chain. This is a string of chain stitches. It's important not to twist the chain, so keep a tight grip on the crocheted chains near your hook.

Tip

The toys are worked in rounds in a continuous spiral. Use a stitch marker to identify the start of each round and move it up as you work.

Working in rounds

All the animals in this book are worked in rounds, in a continuous spiral, so there's no need to close the round after finishing each one of them. This is why the use of stitch markers is vital **(5)**. It's important to mark the beginning of each round with a stitch marker and move this stitch marker up as you work.

Magic ring

Round pieces almost always start with a magic ring, because, when tightened, it will have no holes in the middle where stuffing could come out. To make a magic ring, start in the same way that you would a slip knot, by making a loop shape with the tail end of the yarn. Insert the hook into it and draw another loop of yarn through it. But do not pull the tail end. As well as the loop on your hook, you will have a large loop sitting beneath your hook, with a twisted section of yarn **(6)**. It is important that you work into the centre of the loop for your first round, and also that you work over the twisted section of yarn **(7)**. When you have completed your first round, you can pull the yarn tail tight to close the hole **(8)**.

Attaching heads

Many of the heads in this book are crocheted separately and attached to the body later, especially in the animals that require several colour changes. When you assemble the toy, you will use the long yarn tail left on the last round of the body. First, pin the head in place so it stays in position while you work **(9)**. Then, thread a yarn needle with the long tail or yarn, and join the pieces by working through the stitches on the head and around the neck of the body **(10)**. Make sure you pull the yarn firmly as you sew to avoid wobbly heads and add some extra stuffing before fully joining both pieces together.

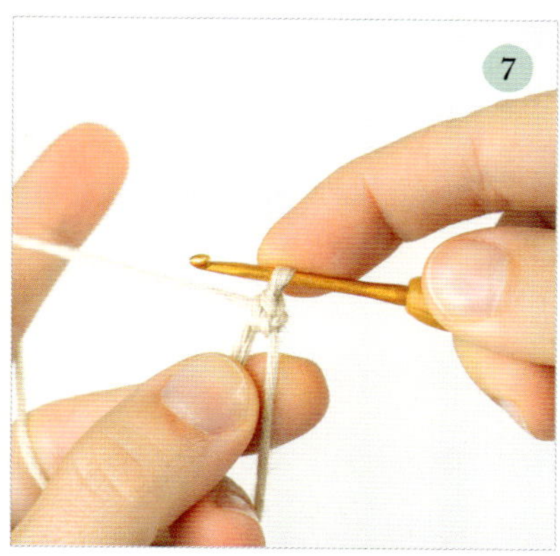

Tip

Master the magic ring to ensure the start of your crochet will be really neat. It may take a little practice but it's worth persevering!

Tip

When the legs present several colour changes, place them facing you when you join the legs. This way, the colour changes will remain at the back of the toy.

Tip

For safety reasons, if you are crocheting the toy for a small child, embroider the eyes with black or dark brown yarn instead of using toy safety eyes.

Joining Legs

Some of the toys in this book, like Tom Kitten, are crocheted from their legs up to the head. To make them, you will crochet one leg first and set it aside while you crochet the second leg. Then, with leg 2 still on your hook, you will make a connecting chain of stitches to join leg 1 with a sc **(1)**. This will be the new beginning of the following rounds, so it's important to place a stitch marker there. You will then have to crochet the rest of the stitches along leg 1 and, after that, work along one side of the chain **(2)**. Then, you will crochet along leg 2 **(3)**, and finally, you will work along the other side of the connecting chain **(4)**. Now you're ready to start the body.

Attaching Eyes

Safety eyes have two parts: the front with a straight or threaded rod, and a washer that goes inside the toy **(5)**. If fastened correctly, it's almost impossible to remove them. You can add a drop of glue to the washer for extra security.

Sewing Cheeks

These are made whilst the head is in progress, after you have attached the safety eyes (if using). Thread a short length of pink onto a yarn needle. Working from the inside of the head, in line with the lower edge of the eye and a few stitches away, make three or four small straight running stitches over two crochet stitches **(6)**, bringing the needle back through to the inside of the head. Fasten off ends.

Closing limbs and ears

The limbs and ears of some of the animals in this book are tube-like pieces and, unless otherwise stated, they do not need to be filled with stuffing. In the last round you will be asked to flatten the opening of the piece, so that the stitches of the top layer align with the stitches of the lower layer **(7)**. Once you've achieved this, join both layers by crocheting 1 sc in each pair of stitches **(8)**. Fasten off, but remember to leave a long yarn tail for sewing to the body **(9)**.

Sewing limbs, tails, and ears

Thread the yarn tail onto a yarn needle and place the piece to be sewn against the body. When you are happy with placement, insert the needle through a stitch on the body **(10)**, and pull the yarn through. Insert the needle through the top of the next stitch on the piece **(11)**, pull yarn through. Repeat this process until the piece is sewn in place **(12)**. Secure the yarn with a few stitches and follow the instructions for Hiding Ends Inside the Toy.

Sewing loose pieces

If required, stuff the piece to be sewn. Thread the yarn needle and position the piece in place. Secure it with pins. Do you like it there? Then let's go **(13)**! Using backstitching, sew the piece with your needle going through under both loops of the last round **(14)**.

Sewing Hair or Hats

Use small straight stitches to sew the piece to the head, working over the sc stitches of the piece **(1)** and making sure that you also work through the stitches of the head, to join them securely. It's OK to space the stitches out as you don't need to work through over every stitch **(2)**. Don't pull the yarn too tightly when sewing, otherwise your stitches may distort the shape of the head. Use matching yarn so that these stitches are not visible.

Creating Armholes on Jackets

Armholes are created over two rows and full instructions are included for each toy's jacket. On the first row, you make a chain of stitches, then skip as many stitches as indicated before working the next sc **(3)**. This creates a chain loop, which is the gap for the armhole. On the next row, you work the stitches into the loops of the chain stitches **(4)** and the armholes are complete.

Edging Flat Pieces

Many of the flat pieces, like the vests that will become jackets, have a crocheted edge to create a neat finish. To do this, you will work as many stitches as instructed in the pattern, working either along the edge and inserting your hook into the spaces between rows **(5)**, or into the stitches themselves **(6)**, depending on which edge you are working along.

Weaving in Ends

With the wrong side of your piece facing, thread the tail end onto a yarn needle and insert the needle underneath the posts of three or four stitches **(7)**. Pull the yarn through and snip close to the work **(8)**. If you feel it necessary, you can repeat this process by working back through the same stitches: skip the first stitch and then insert your needle underneath the next few stitches. Pull yarn through and snip yarn close to the work.

Creating sleeves

Most of the jackets in this book are really vests which, together with the arms, will look like jackets. They are not meant to be removed once you've assembled the character. Peter Rabbit, Benjamin Bunny and Tom Kitten often lose their clothes while making mischief, so their jackets have sleeves and can be taken off and put on as many times as you like! While the vest-piece of the jackets is worked in rows, the sleeves are crocheted in rounds, so use a stitch marker to keep your place. To start each sleeve, you will join the yarn to the outside of one of the chain stitches you made when creating the armhole **(9)**. Then you will continue crocheting along the remaining chain stitches **(10)** and, finally, into the stitches that you skipped when you created the armhole **(11)**. Then continue crocheting in rounds. Don't forget to use a stitch marker!

Tip

Before fastening off the sleeve, check against your toy to see if you are satisfied with the length. If not, simply add an extra round or two.

Some additional notes

The bodies of these characters, and most of their limbs and accessories, are crocheted by working in a spiral.

Remember to mark the beginning of each round with a stitch marker. There is no need to close each round with a slip stitch.

When changing colours, you'll get a 'step' in the fabric and yes, we all hate it. There is no way to avoid it though, so embrace it and try to place it at the back of your toys!

I usually use bits of pink yarn to embroider the cheeks of the animals, but you can also opt for fabric blushes or markers.

Can I wash these toys? Yes, you can! If you only want to remove a small stain, just dampen the area with a wet cloth and a bit of soap. If you want to wash the toy completely, place it in the washing machine: gentle cycle and tumble dry low. Warning: some colours might fade just a bit.

About the Author

Hello everyone! I'm glad to see you again in this new crochet adventure! In case this is our first journey together, my name is Carla Mitrani and I live in Buenos Aires, Argentina. I am married to Nachi and we have two sons, Iñaki and Homero, and a small dog, called Peppa. Learning to crochet has absolutely changed my world: I've discovered a new way to express myself, invent cuddly friends and mostly unwind... It's the best therapy ever! You can follow my crochet adventures on Instagram: @amourfou_crochet.

This is my fourth book of crochet patterns with my friends at David and Charles. But this book was a huge challenge, because these characters are not the result of my imagination but of Beatrix Potter's beautiful paintings and I had to be true to them. I tried to honour her artistic vision and I sincerely hope that she would approve, and that you will enjoy making them.

Acknowledgements

In January 2024, Ame Verso approached me with the *Peter Rabbit™ Crochet Toys* project. I have been living in a dream since then. Ame, what can I say? No words can express my gratitude. I am still in awe that my life will forever be intertwined with Beatrix Potter's characters. Thank you from the bottom of my heart! And special thanks to Frederick Warne for allowing me to be part of this project and green-lighting my take on Beatrix Potter's beautiful characters.

This book was also special because I got to work again with Lucy Ridley and Jason Jenkins, who I now think of as lifelong friends. I love going to Exeter, Devon, to work with you, talk about our lives, our children and how we celebrate Christmas. You are the best, guys!

I must tell my mother that I was separated at birth from Marie Clayton. We were so in tune during the technical editing stage that we kept joking we were sisters. I owe you a lot Marie!

Of course, none of that would have been possible without Rachael Prest, who did the first technical edit, finding all the first typos and mistakes and making our work easier. Jess Cropper: thank you so much for overseeing all of us and making all this come to life!

I would also love to thank all the team at David and Charles for receiving me with such warmth and kindness. It's always a pleasure to see you all.

I could not have finished this book without the love and support (and extreme patience) of my dear family, especially my husband and my children. Thank you so much for believing in me! A special thanks to my mom, Liliana, for being the first one to see each finished toy and giving me honest feedback. All the characters that made it to this book were first officially approved by her. I love you!

INDEX

A DAVID AND CHARLES BOOK

David and Charles is an imprint of David and Charles, Ltd, Suite A, Tourism House, Pynes Hill, Exeter, EX2 5WS

First published in the UK and USA in 2025

A catalogue record for this book is available from the British Library.

ISBN-13: 9781446315798 paperback
ISBN-13: 9781446315811 EPUB

This book has been printed on paper from approved suppliers and made from pulp from sustainable sources.

Printed in China through Asia Pacific Offset for: David and Charles, Ltd, Suite A, Tourism House, Pynes Hill, Exeter, EX2 5WS

10 9 8 7 6 5 4 3 2 1

Publishing Director: Ame Verso
Publishing Manager: Jeni Chown
Editor: Jessica Cropper
Project Editor: Marie Clayton
Lead Designer: Sam Staddon
Design and Art Direction: Lucy Ridley
Pre-press Designer: Susan Reansbury
Technique Illustrations: Kuo Kang Chen
Photography: Jason Jenkins, Carla Mitrani (page 5)
Production Manager: Beverley Richardson

David and Charles publishes high-quality books on a wide range of subjects. For more information visit www.davidandcharles.com.

Share your makes with us on social media using #dandcbooks and follow us on Facebook and Instagram by searching for @dandcbooks.

Layout of the digital edition of this book may vary depending on reader hardware and display settings.